W9-DBE-067

# THE WILDERNESS TATTOO

# THE WILDERNESS TATTOO

A NARRATIVE OF JUAN ORTIZ

by

William O. Steele

*Illustrated with old prints*

NEW YORK

HARCOURT BRACE JOVANOVICH, INC.

Copyright © 1972 by William O. Steele

ISBN 0-15-297325-7

Library of Congress Catalog Card Number: 77-167838

Printed in the United States of America

First edition

B C D E F G H I J

*To my mother-in-law,*
CHRISTINE NOBLE GOVAN,
*for sharing her shingles*

# CONTENTS

*The story can be followed by reading the
numbered titled chapters.*

*Background material for the narrative and
historical comment are in
the* INTERLUDES.

AUTHOR'S NOTE                                11

CHAPTER   1   The Death's Head Cacique       17

             INTERLUDE I                     23

          2   Spanish Barbecue               27
          3   New World Slave                32

             INTERLUDE II                    37

          4   Guard of the Dead              41
          5   Farewell, Acuera               45
          6   A Brief Sweet Taste of Freedom 49
          7   A Christian Becomes a Savage   53

             INTERLUDE III                   59

9

# Contents

8    The Broken Cross    64

9    A Strange Plague    70

INTERLUDE IV    77

10    Sneak Attack    83

11    War Against the Calusans    90

INTERLUDE V    97

12    Shining Conquistadors    103

13    Adelantado of Florida    109

INTERLUDE VI    115

14    The New World Interpreter    118

15    Mocoço's Visit    125

INTERLUDE VII    131

16    First Adventures    139

17    Loose Spanish Teeth    146

18    Winter Quarters in Apalache    153

19    A Battle for a Bed    160

20    Two Heads Saved    170

INTERLUDE VIII    177

OBITUARY    181

SELECTED BIBLIOGRAPHY    183

## Author's Note

All that is known of Juan Ortiz in the New World comes from four sources, the four accounts of the De Soto Expedition. The authors of three of these were members of the expedition; the fourth (The Inca, Garcilaso de la Vega) interviewed survivors of the expedition to write his history.

There is much disagreement among these chroniclers, not only about the incidents concerning Ortiz but also every aspect of the expedition, so only the most reasonable episodes have been selected for this narrative.

The four accounts are listed in the bibliography.

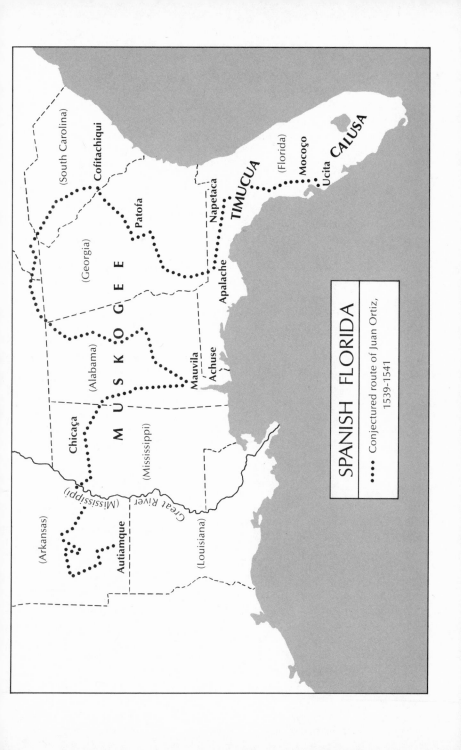

SPANISH FLORIDA

•••••• Conjectured route of Juan Ortiz,
1539-1541

CALUSA

(Florida)

Mocoço

Ucita

TIMUCUA

Napetaca

Apalache

Cofitachiqui

(South Carolina)

Patofa

(Georgia)

M U S K O G E E

(Alabama)

Mauvila

Achuse

Chicaça

(Mississippi)

Great River (Mississippi!)

(Arkansas)

Autiamque

(Louisiana)

# THE WILDERNESS TATTOO

# The Death's Head Cacique

Juan Ortiz raced his three shipmates across the burning Florida sands. Just ahead was the prize—a letter held in the split end of an upright cane. Suddenly there was a rasping metallic shriek from over the water of the bay.

Juan whirled and stared in horror. The anchor of the Spanish brigantine was being hauled up. The chain clanked, and the sails flapped into place and filled. The other three Spaniards ran back toward the water screaming, but slowly the brigantine rocked toward the open sea.

"Don't leave us here!" cried Juan. "Holy Mother! Don't leave us to the savages!"

He sank to his knees and reached out a pleading hand. Groans of despair came from deep within him. His body trembled. The brigantine sailed on.

Naked men raced from their hiding places and seized the sailors. Juan's captor dragged him to his feet and brought his face close to the boy's. The face was dark and stained with paint and scarred with tattoo marks.

Juan shrank from the cruel look. How could the others have deserted them? How could they have left their comrades in the hands of these wild merciless savages? How could Christians abandon fellow Christians to infidels?

The Indian shoved him up the beach to join the others. The four captives dared not look at each other as they were herded along in the soft sand. Each was fearful enough without taking on the fears of the others. Each had no doubt that he would soon be horribly dead, for these natives were well known to the Spaniards of the New World for their cruelty.

Juan Ortiz prayed as he was pushed this way and that through the tangle of vines and scrawny palms. He prayed not to live—there was no hope of that—but to die bravely as befitted a Christian and a Spaniard. From the tales he had heard of these savages, he would need more courage than he could muster without the help of saints and angels and the Virgin Mother herself. The other three were older men. They would not like to hear their companion behave like a coward and scream and plead for mercy.

They came to a scattering of thatched and miserable huts. One of the Indians gave a loud whoop. The villagers poured out of their dwellings. Each had some kind of weapon. Even the smallest children tottered toward the captives with jagged pieces of shell. The Spaniards hesitated, and their captors drove them forward into the mob. They were poked at and struck, slashed and jabbed by men, women, and screaming youths. The four whites crowded together, warding off the blows as best they could.

As they neared a mound of dirt, the villagers fell away and quieted. A dwelling finer and larger than the others perched on the flat top of the mound. Before it a thin man sat cross-legged. An Indian woman fanned him, another rubbed oil on his body, while others placed vessels of food around him. He must surely be a cacique, a chieftain.

A quick jab of flint knives sent the Spaniards struggling up the slope to stand before this important one. He gave them a sweeping disdainful glance without pausing in his meal.

Juan stared at him with horrified fascination, for his nose had been cut off, leaving only a little red-rimmed hole. His eyes seemed gone, too, so deep set and dark were they in the face that was little more than skin and bone. He looked like a death's head, a skeleton skull set on a still-fleshed body.

At last he stopped eating. Looking directly at Juan, he said a few words and motioned to have the prisoner taken away. At once the boy's captor hurried him down the slope and through the village to an empty hut. He was flung inside and a guard placed in the doorless entrance. The youth lay where he fell, too tired and sore, frightened and dispirited to do more. There was no way to tell how long he lay there on the dirt floor before he heard screams of pain and the joyful answering cries of the Indians.

He jerked upright. His companions' shrieks went on.

He could not make himself look out the door. Instead, he covered his ears with his hands and put his head on his drawn-up knees. The torture must indeed be awful to bring such inhuman sounds from his brave companions.

How quickly their fortunes had shifted. That very morning the four of them had sat at the brigantine's railing talking of the riches Pánfilo de Narváez, newly appointed Governor of Florida, would find and share with all of his followers. They had reached the bay where part of their expedition, led by de Narváez, had gone ashore earlier. The beach curved like a sickle moon around them. In the middle of the beach stood an upright cane holding something that shone like a bleached bone. All on board were sure it was a letter of instructions from their leader, Narváez, for which they had been searching.

Yet, no one wanted to go fetch it back to the ship. Indians roamed among the trees. There were very few soldiers aboard the brigantine, not nearly enough to fight the savages in case they attacked any party sent for the letter. There was nothing to do but drop anchor and wait.

After a while, a pirogue full of Indians had paddled out to the ship. By signs they asked the Spaniards to take the letter away. There were strange symbols on the outside of the paper. Evil hovered around it. They were scared to touch it. They begged the white men to take it away before their town and lands fell under its dreadful spell.

Still no one wanted to risk his life for the letter. The natives were not to be trusted. At last the Indians offered to leave hostages on the ship. It had seemed a trustworthy offer to Juan Ortiz. He and his three friends volunteered.

How the sailors had laughed and joked as the four clambered down the side of the ship into the pirogue. How blue the bay had been under the bright sun, how lush and green the growth behind the beach. All was peaceful and quiet, and the letter was so close, so easily obtained.

Then the treachery happened. Suddenly the beach was dark with Indian figures. The hostages had escaped from the brigantine, and the ship sailed away at once without even trying to rescue the four Spaniards.

In the hut Juan waited through the afternoon in tense terror. Any moment the savages would surely come for him. But no. The sun sank lower, the guard's shadow grew longer, and still he stayed there. The town was unusually quiet. Had the torture ended? Had the townspeople gone to their houses for the coming night?

He got stiffly to his feet and gazed fearfully out the doorway. At one side of the plaza sat the cacique with his archers around him. At a gesture from him one of the Indians notched a long, slender arrow to his bowstring and shot.

Juan couldn't follow the arrow's flight without shifting his position, but he didn't move. He had no desire to see what was shot at. He waited, expecting a scream as the dart found its mark. But there was no cry. It puzzled Juan. He dreaded to look, but he had to know what was happening.

He moved a step, and what he saw made him suck in his breath harshly. A blood-smeared, dirty, naked figure tottered dazedly about the open square. His arms and legs and shoulders were pricked with countless arrows. Barbed and feathered ends stuck out at odd angles and flapped loosely with each step. Only one dart had pierced his body, and this was low in his right side. The Spaniard tugged constantly at it, but his efforts were weak and fumbling. He stumbled on.

The savages were shooting not to kill but to wound the Spaniard and keep him alive for an afternoon of sport. It seemed impossible that a human so full of arrows could still keep going, but whichever one of his friends this was managed to stumble on. The other two lay in the center of the square, bloody lumps of flesh and feathered darts, their torture mercifully ended for all time.

Juan turned away, sick and hopeless, and threw himself on the ground. Bad enough to die abandoned in this strange, bizarre land, without friend or relative or priest to touch his hand or offer him any comfort. But to die so horribly!

What did gold matter now, or great adventure, or noble purpose? He groaned and began to pray with all his will.

# INTERLUDE I

Juan Ortiz lived at a time of great excitement in Spain —the dawning years of the sixteenth century.

The last of the Moslem conquerors had been driven from the Spanish peninsula. It had taken eight hundred years and three thousand battles to accomplish this. Now the country was free. But for so long all the strength and imagination of the country had been turned toward fighting and struggling. The Spanish people seemed now to be looking for some new outlet, some new world to conquer.

And then Christopher Columbus came to their aid, with a whole new world indeed. Fourteen ninety-two, and the falling-off edge of the western sea they had always believed in was softened into a horizon dotted with islands and terrae firmae. The Indies? The Antilles? The legendary island of Brazil? It mattered not. The Admiral of the Ocean Sea had burst through the unknown and the darkness and swept away forever the lurking watery horrors of the Atlantic Ocean from men's minds. A new-found land lay to the west of Europe. And it belonged to Spain.

23

The Spanish people were stirred to a frenzy by Columbus's four voyages across the Atlantic. Many sailed after him and added to his discoveries and returned home with much to tell.

They brought back strange names that shone with a new glamor and sang a siren song. Island of Bimini. Cuba. Isthmus of Panama. Chicora. Bahia Honda. Yucatan.

They brought back tale upon tale. Green islands of paradise floating on blue seas. Dusty Indian maidens of rare beauty. Golden cities. Mountains of silver.

Soon the New World was the commonest subject of gossip in the Spanish markets and became the talk of the wealthy in castle halls. Tales of riches and romance were repeated in monasteries as often as prayers and daily concerned the Spanish monarch and his royal priests and scholars.

There was no stopping the Spaniards. Swordsmen, nobles, cavaliers, women, officials, Dominican and Franciscan priests—all were feverish to sail westward. Eyes yearned for strange faraway sights. Fingers twitched for the smooth feel of precious stones, for the heavy delight of gold. Souls throbbed to carry to the heathen Indians the belief in the one true God above.

A steady stream embarked from Spanish ports, spread over the islands of the Caribbean Sea, and flooded to the surrounding mainlands of the Americas. Lands were conquered for the glory of God and the chance to get rich.

At first very little gold or silver or treasure of jewels was discovered. But the lands of the New World had a wealth of another kind—natives. Docile Indians were easily captured and quickly sold as slaves. Spaniards grew wealthy from the slave trade. Island after island was drained of natives. More had to be found to clear jungles for plantations, to build houses and churches and roadways.

The Spanish Crown was shocked at the idea of slavery in their New World colonies. The enslavement of Indians was forbidden unless such Indians were captured in "a just war." But what was "a just war"? Who could decide such a question? Neither king nor priest. Slave hunting continued as a just war against all savages.

The Crown proclaimed that cannibals might be seized at any time. Their seizure was a noble act. After all, if heathen cannibals were brought into the services of Christians, they might be more easily converted to the Holy Catholic faith. Suddenly cannibals lurked in every corner of the New World, swarmed in the jungles, infested the mountains. Every Indian was considered a flesh-eater. Spaniards sailed in all directions to root out these infidels.

It was during a slave-hunting expedition that Ponce de Leon chanced upon a new land in 1513. Since he found no natives along the coast to capture, he had time to bestow a name. Because there were many sweet-scented flowering trees and shrubs and because it was Easter Sunday, *Pascua Florida*, he called it Tierra Florida. Later, he tried to colonize his Florida but was killed by an Indian arrow.

Florida waited, tempting, beautiful, and lush—empty

of Christians, but perhaps filled with treasure hoards. Pánfilo de Narváez, a Spanish soldier and adventurer, felt the magnetic possibilities of the land. He came to desire it with all his heart. So the Spanish Crown granted him a patent to explore Florida, to limn its dimensions, and to colonize it. However, a percentage of all treasures found must go into the royal coffers. The terms granted were the usual ones, written to make every one a winner.

Narváez sailed from Spain in June 1527 with approximately six hundred men in five ships. With him was the seventeen-year-old Juan Ortiz. By April of the following year the expedition reached Tampa Bay on the west coast of Florida. Here Narváez split up his followers. A part went inland with him. The rest were to explore the coastline and look for instructions he would leave them.

It was one of Narváez's brigantines that later returned to Tampa Bay where Juan Ortiz and his three friends were lured ashore with a letter placed there by the Indians. Those men safe on the ship felt *burlados*, laughed at, wrote a chronicler. They were civilized Spaniards, proud Christians, humiliated and tricked by ignorant savages. It was an incident they wanted to forget and put forever out of their minds. They did— quickly, easily—by sailing away and leaving their four shipmates in the hands of the naked Floridians.

Thus it came about that Juan Ortiz shed his commonplace yesteryears and stepped forth into history as a New World pioneer.

# CHAPTER TWO

# Spanish Barbecue

The night was endless. Though there was a full moon, it cast a pale and deathly light. The village was quiet, but numerous night creatures stirred and called to each other with strange sad cries.

Juan lay in the rubbish on the floor of the hut but couldn't sleep. He tried sitting upright like the snoring guard. Still his eyelids wouldn't stay shut. Rest was impossible. He was much too uneasy. What lay ahead for him tomorrow? What torture had the noseless savage cacique devised for him to suffer? He mourned and thrashed about. It was a maddening enough torture merely to wait for tomorrow's agony.

Something rattled about in the dry reed roof. Then a huge hairy spider slipped down the wall, hurried across the floor, and leaped over the sleeping guard's feet and was gone.

How easily it had gotten away! Could he not do the same and hide on the beach till another ship appeared? He got to his feet and tiptoed to the doorway. At once the guard's snores ceased, and two alert eyes were on him. He sat back down. It was no use. Anyway, there would be no way to hide from these natives. It was told they could sniff out a trail as well as any Spanish dog. Escape was hopeless.

The moon melted into the dark line of trees beyond the village. Leaves rustled in the dimness, and a cool, musty smell of ocean and mud flats filled the hut. A moment later the sun was up, all too soon, and heat squiggles danced through the town.

There was much activity throughout the village. Juan watched as men and women hastened about the streets and small groups of heavily armed warriors headed for the jungles. On the mound stood the cacique, calling out to those passing below. He walked slowly around the top of the mound, watching everything. Then he stopped and stared straight at Juan in the doorway. The youth shrank back, trembling.

The guard moved into the shade of the hut and ate breakfast. Nothing was offered Juan, but he didn't mind. Though he had had no food or drink since leaving the brigantine, terror had banished hunger and thirst. Every warrior crossing the square toward the hut frightened him into believing the time to die had finally arrived. Yet, the morning passed and no one came for him.

Through the afternoon, hunters returned and carried their kill to great cooking fires at the edge of town. Others came in with big sea turtles and baskets of fish. The village was preparing for some celebration. What part would the Spanish prisoner play?

He dozed often, waking with fear at some loud noise

or call. Once he awoke and found a gourd of water and a bowl of stewed meat and roots inside the door. The day was ending, and he was still alive. He was ready to eat.

All night long the town's preparations went on. Fires were everywhere. No one seemed to go to bed. Juan went to sleep at last with the aroma of roasting meat in his nostrils.

Breakfast was something peculiar and bitter, but he ate with appetite. He noticed that an open arbor with a palmetto-thatch roof had been erected during the night at the foot of the mound. Already the villagers were gathering about it.

Soon the cacique left his dwelling and moved down the mound steps. On his head was the skin of a white bird, its wings extended to each side. The bird's great beak rested on the chieftain's forehead. He wore a short fur mantle and a breechclout decorated with pearls. Behind him came his wife and children, all richly attired.

A servant placed a wooden stool under the arbor, and the cacique sat and stared about him with regal arrogance. On his right were his finely dressed advisers, to his left his family and court women. Armed guards stood in back of them.

At a sign from the cacique, a native raised a conch shell to his lips and blew. As the sound died, an Indian in painted skins and fancy boots appeared at the far end of the plaza. With slow, stately steps the cacique advanced, followed by bearers with loaded baskets on their shoulders. These baskets were placed on the

ground before the noseless chieftain and were inspected by him. They met with his approval, and he
ordered them taken to his dwelling. The newcomer
bowed and stood to one side.

Again the conch shell blared, and another well-
dressed cacique crossed the square with his train of
servants bearing presents. It could have been the King
of Spain receiving tribute from his noble subjects, such
great pomp and ceremony did the Floridians follow.
Who would have guessed these New World savages
would have such a civilized occasion?

Throughout the morning the subject caciques paid
their tributes to their leader. The offering of one was
not acceptable. The noseless cacique ordered him pun-
ished. Guards held him while another broke his right
arm with a wooden club. There was no cry from the of-
fender, no sign of pain on his face. He bowed to his
leader and with his followers walked regally away between the huts.

At last the ceremony was over. The head cacique
stood and gave a speech. Suddenly two guards broke
out of the crowd and ran toward Juan's hut. The youth
shrank back against the wall, biting his lips and moaning softly. His time of doom had arrived.

The guards entered and quickly stripped off his
clothes. Then, grabbing him by the arms, they dragged
him across the square to the far side, where a bed of
wood embers glowed under a crisscrossed rack of green
canes, a *barbacoa*.

Juan struggled, but it was useless. The guards spread
him on the *barbacoa* on his back and tied his arms and

legs to posts at each corner. The heat began to scorch his flesh. He screamed and begged for mercy, but not a cruel eye blinked, not a dark wooden face was moved by his cries.

Juan Ortiz was being roasted alive, barbecued on the *barbacoa.*

᠍᠍

# CHAPTER THREE

# New World Slave

The heat grew more and more intense. Juan tried to arch his body away from it, but he was tied too tightly. The searing pain burned deeper. The whole world was on fire. He screamed his prayers aloud to give him courage.

"Hail Mary . . . be with me now . . . at this hour of death!"

Suddenly a young girl dashed from the group of women around the cacique. With a flint knife she slashed the thongs and pulled Juan from the *barbacoa* and laid him face down on the ground. His legs and buttocks were streaked black and red, like charred meat. Great round blisters, like the pulpy insides of halved oranges, covered his back.

Juan saw the girl kneeling at his side before he fainted from a world of red agony into cool darkness.

When he came to himself, he was in a kind of shed. He lay on a raised couch on a pallet of skins. The slightest movement sent pain racing through him. After a while the girl who had saved him came in with an older woman. They applied a salve to his back. Juan could tell they were mother and daughter by their strong resemblance. The salve helped, and later he managed to raise his head and shoulders enough to suck hot liquid through a piece of hollow cane.

The weeks went by, and Juan's wounds slowly healed. The burns had been deep and left great scars that drew his skin painfully. But he was glad to be alive. As soon as his head cleared of fever, he tried to thank the women for saving his life. They smiled as if they understood his Spanish words.

In time he was able to stand up, but walking was still very painful for him. The girl visited him daily to doctor the burns with various herbs and ointments and to teach him her language. She was a patient teacher and kept Juan struggling with the words, though they stuck to his tongue like so many burrs.

Her name was Acuera, and she was the daughter of Ucita, a Timucuan cacique who controlled many of the surrounding towns.

"I could not bear to see you burned," Acuera told the boy. "And I begged for your life. Then my mother pointed out that Ucita had nothing to fear from one so young as you and that, while one Spaniard might do no good, he could certainly do little harm."

"Be sure to thank your mother again for me," Juan said in halting phrases.

"I said it would be an honor for a cacique to have a Spanish slave," Acuera continued. "My father agreed to spare your life and let us doctor you."

She clasped her hands tightly together, and her

voice grew sad. "Now I fear your life will be only a living death, for my father has recently suffered many indignities at the hands of your countrymen and hates you and all Spaniards."

She recounted how a great many men had disembarked from huge ships in the nearby bay. They had captured her father and sliced off his nose and killed and dismembered her grandmother.

Juan sighed. It must have been his erstwhile commander—Narváez—who had done this dreadful thing. And now he, Juan Ortiz, not Narváez, must suffer the consequences.

It was the last time Acuera came to his hut. And her warning proved correct. Ucita turned up in her place and personally saw that his Spanish slave was set to the most unwanted and dirtiest chores in the village. In between the hard tasks he worked unceasingly at fetching and carrying and at gathering the stiff spiky palmetto leaves used to thatch roofs.

Juan came to dread most the days when Ucita watched him, fingering the red scarred bit of his nose. Then the Indian's face twisted with rage and his black eyes burned with hatred. Was it simply Narváez's cruelty that had made Ucita so cruel and vengeful? Or were all the Indians in this land like that? In the islands of the Indies the natives, though infidels, were not like these merciless savages.

Except for the infrequent times when Acuera and her mother spoke to him, Juan received only jeers and taunts from the other villagers. No one came near him except to strike him with a fist or club or to nick him with a spear or knife. His body was continually bruised and scabbed.

But worse than the blows was the knowledge that at any time Ucita might kill him. Every morning Juan opened his eyes and wondered if today was the day when he would be burned again or cut into little pieces or slowly strangled for Ucita's pleasure.

The fall winds blew themselves out, the short winter calmed the earth, the spring rains fell and disappeared, and another summer of ceaseless work came for Juan. He feared he would not be able to last much longer in this new world, would never live to see Sevilla and his beloved Spain.

# INTERLUDE II

Acuera—young, pretty, perhaps tattoed to enhance her beauty, wearing a short apron, her hair silky black and loose and long down her back. Here is the first southern belle in the history of the New World—a Timucuan Indian.

Why would she save Juan Ortiz from burning? For his curling hair and young good looks? Out of curiosity and desire for a closer look at this strange new creature? Compassion? Who knows? But she saved his life.

Here is the prototype of the romantic rescue of Captain John Smith by Pocahontas, daughter of an Indian chieftain of Virginia. Across the American continent other Indian women were to step forth and save a white man's life time and again. Pocahontas's rescue was the most famous of all these. But Acuera's was the very first.

The Timucuans inhabited the central and northern sections of the Florida peninsula. A Frenchman who lived among East Coast Timucuans described them as "of good stature, well shaped of body as any people in

the world; very generous, courteous and good na-
tured."

Scholars say the Timucuan language has a distinc-
tiveness all its own, a language different from any
other of the United States. "Timucua" comes from the
word "ati-muca," which literally means "servants at-
tend upon him," but a better translation is "master" or
"ruler." Surely such a lordly appellation is deserved by
these Indians.

The Spanish called any Indian leader a cacique. The
Timucuan caciques had a great deal more civil and
military authority than other tribal chieftains of southeastern America, no matter how many or how few
towns were under their control.

It is debated whether the chieftain gave his name to
a province that he controlled and to his own town, or
whether the cacique took his name from the province
or town. It made little difference to the Spanish in
their careless use of Timucuan terms. Ocita, also
spelled Ucita, was the town where Juan Ortiz was a
slave, as well as the name given to its leader by the
Spanish chroniclers. The town is believed to have been
located in the southeastern portion of Tampa Bay, perhaps on Terra Ceia Island.

Some idea of the Timucuan home life and ceremonies can be found in a few French Huguenot narratives
and from the pictorial illustrations of the French artist,
Jacques le Moyne. Knowledge of their language, customs, and beliefs comes from the catechisms, the
grammar, and the dictionary of Francisco Pareua, a

Spanish missionary who lived among the Timucuans for sixteen years in the vicinity of St. Augustine in northeast Florida.

The Timucuans were an agricultural people. However, they depended more on game, fish, oysters, wild fruits, and the bread made from two different wild plant roots than on what they raised in their gardens. It has been noted that in times of dire necessity they ate "a thousand riffraffs"—coal, dirt, broken pottery, fleas, and lice. And a feast of human flesh was not turned down if they felt like indulging in it.

Scalping and mutilation of the dead were practiced. Human sacrifice was at times a part of their religious ceremony. They wore few clothes, greased their bodies, and occasionally adorned themselves in basket hats. Some painted the skin around their mouths blue.

Of all the different tribes of Indians the Europeans encountered across the North American continent, the Timucuans are unique in one respect—they could steal with both their feet and their hands. Their neighbors, the French, said so and labeled them the "greatest thieves in the world," observing that they stole without conscience and claimed as their very own all they carried away secretly. But the gallant Frenchmen added in their accounts that the comely Timucuan women did not steal at all.

Timucuans were no more warlike and cruel than other southeastern tribes, nor than their Spanish opponents. It was a cruel age in Europe in the sixteenth century, and the thousands of people in the cities who flocked to see a criminal tortured were no better than the Indians watching an enemy tormented in their public square.

The Europeans were given a rough reception time and again by the Timucuans. Although some of these Indians became Christians under Spanish domination in the 1600's, nevertheless the pressures of encroaching white civilization eventually were too much for them, and they finally vanished from the peninsula of Florida and the pages of history.

# CHAPTER FOUR

# Guard of the Dead

Juan had never ceased his daily prayers since his capture. His faith was sincere, deep. It had always been. Now he prayed with more earnestness than ever before. He prayed to be worthy of a miracle from God. He asked to be taken away from the Timucuans, to be delivered out of the hands of the infidels.

It could not be by his own hand. That was against his religion. No true Christian would do such a thing, lest his soul be lost forever among the dammed.

Yet nights found him with a cane knife at hand. Its sharp, thin blade could reach his heart quickly with one stab. He prayed to resist this temptation; and that of the ever-present shells with edges sharp enough to slash the flesh of the throat; and the leather thongs with their easily made noose of choking death. He prayed against all of these.

Daytimes he prayed aloud as he dragged himself through the swamps, as his numb fingers broke open oysters, as he cut wood with a stone ax whose blade edge was as thick as his hand. He prayed and struggled always to do whatever was commanded of him, in spite of pain and fear, weariness and grief.

One afternoon as he was finishing his day's work, he was summoned to Ucita. He followed the messenger out of the village along a path through the dense forest. The way was endless. He was half dead with fatigue and stumbled and fell often. But he forced himself to his feet and stumbled to keep up with the Indian guide. At last they arrived at a clearing.

Ucita and three of his advisers stood waiting. In the glow of the sunset their long shadows stretched toward him, weird and black. Behind them in the center of the open place stood a building. Juan had never seen it before and did not know what it was. It could not be a dwelling, for there was a strangeness about it and a horrifying smell. Even Ucita looked about uneasily. Hurriedly Juan crossed himself.

"You are to guard the Temple of the Dead," the cacique said. "My grandson is resting here now."

All yesterday Juan had heard the wails of the mourners. He had even glimpsed a part of the burial procession leaving the village but had paid little heed to it.

"A body has been taken from the temple recently," Ucita went on. "It is not right that the dead should be disturbed." He took the messenger's spear and handed it to the slave. "Take this. Guard my grandson well, else I will torture you with my own two hands."

Ucita ran his finger along the scar of his nose. A vicious smile touched his lips. Juan shuddered.

"When the sun returns, I will return. Make sure that when I come, I will be pleased at all things here."

The Indians went away quickly. Darkness surged softly in from the trees. Three great white herons flapped over the clearing. Juan watched them settle in the top of a tree behind the temple. White as ghosts, they gleamed through the dusk.

He looked in the door of the temple. There were benches supporting cane coffins. The lids were loose slabs of bark. He made out the small box holding the cacique's tiny grandson. Everything was safe and quiet. Nothing stirred here. The dead slept peacefully.

A long mourning cry made him whirl around, his spear lowered before him. He saw nothing. The herons had left their treetop. It was some other bird, then, calling in the gloom. Or—or a lost soul? This was, after all, a burial place, and certainly not a sanctified one for Christian men. A soul in torment might make a moan much as Juan had heard. Juan trembled.

He glanced into the place of the dead, but he dared not go inside. The last light faded from the sky, and finally he sat by the doorway with his back against the wall and prayed. There were other strange noises from the jungle, each more ghastly than the last. He gripped his spear tightly and prayed once again for strength and courage.

At last the night grew quiet, and Juan found it hard to stay awake. He was tired, so very tired. His bones ached. His lids fell over his eyes in spite of everything he could do. He dropped the spear and lay on the ground. He would not sleep but only rest there awhile.

He came awake with a jerk, staring around in the darkness. What was that sound? He sprang to his feet, seizing the spear, and then darted into the temple. Feeling around in the dark, he found Ucita's grandson's box. It was tumbled to the floor—empty!

He looked toward the rear doorway in time to see a great dark shape silhouetted against the starlit night. With a yell he ran forward between the coffins. The creature was gone. He heard it moving off into the undergrowth. Whatever it was, it could not go far or fast carrying the child's body. And wherever it went, he must follow or die. He plunged in after it.

From ahead came a growl that swelled into a roar which was half a scream. A panther! He paused uneasily. Yet he must go on. If the panther made away with the body, the fate that awaited him at Ucita's hands would be far worse than a fight in the dark with this murderous beast.

He edged slowly forward, pushing through the bushes with care and stopping at intervals to listen. A quick, soft padding step sounded behind him. He whirled but in the blackness could see nothing. There was a crackling to one side. The panther was circling him, closing in to spring. Juan gripped the spear with both hands and backed up against a tree. A good hard thrust with the weapon would be his only chance.

He waited and watched. Was that the gleam of eyes now on this side, now on that? It must be a panther and its mate. Against two he had no chance whatsoever. Suddenly the bushes in front of him rustled. A hulking shape loomed blacker than the shadows. Juan raised his spear. For a moment he was almost paralyzed with fear and despair. And then he threw with all his might!

# CHAPTER FIVE

# Farewell, Acuera

There was not a sound. He huddled against the tree and waited, trembling. Nothing! No sound, no movement, only the rolling blackness of the jungle. Where was the panther? He had missed, and now it was creeping slowly toward him on quiet feet. He would not know where it was until its claws ripped through his body. He was lost and terribly cold. All warmth, his very blood, life itself seemed to drain out of him. He fell forward on his face, and a dark tide swept over him.

The sound of voices woke him. It was daylight. Juan jumped to his feet, shaking all over. He must run and hide before Ucita found him here. The panther had not killed him, but surely the Timucuan cacique would.

It was too late. The savages had already surrounded him. One burst through the underbrush and grabbed him. "Here is the faithless one," the warrior cried. "He was trying to escape. He deserves the worst of tortures."

Ucita strode angrily through the trees, and already

his furious hands were reaching out to seize the Spaniard. But before the cacique could do more than grab Juan's arm, one of the others cried out and pointed. To one side in a pathetic little heap lay the chieftain's grandson. Beside the child was an enormous panther with Juan's spear driven straight through it.

Slowly the Indian released the Spaniard's arm and turned on him a brief admiring glance. Juan staggered back weakly. Once again he was saved. God above was watching over him.

"In the dark!" murmured one. "He killed the panther in the blackness of night!"

Life was somewhat better after that for Juan. He received more food, and some days passed when he was given only a few clouts by the villagers he served. But this did not last. Ucita had not forgotten his hatred. The tasks became harder again. Juan was beaten, starved, and reviled more than ever.

Once he spent a day in useless trotting back and forth across the square from dawn till the sun set. The cacique watched while his bowmen stood ready to shoot the Spaniard the instant he stopped; the sun beat down, Juan's throat and mouth dried to where he could scarcely swallow, his legs cramped and shook with weariness. Yet he did not fall. At dusk Ucita suddenly quit the square; the bowmen turned their eyes away from Juan. Once more he had lived through a day that as easily as not might have been his last.

One night as he lay sleeping under a small brush arbor he had made himself, he was awakened by a shake of his shoulder. He started up, and a hand slid over his mouth. Acuera whispered in his ear, "Don't make a sound. You must leave at once. Tomorrow my father will sacrifice you, for our god is thirsty for blood."

"Where can I possibly go that Ucita cannot find me?" Juan asked softly.

"The cacique of the next province loves me and wants to take me as his wife," she replied. "Tell him I sent you and that I demand he protect you."

Juan had no possessions to take with him but the breechclout he was wearing and a cane knife. Acuera led him around the huts and out past the town guard into the forest. There an old man waited.

"I can go no farther," she said. "This man I trust. He will guide you to the province of Mocoço. Farewell for now, white one."

"Acuera, I thank you a thousand times over," Juan told her. "I will never forget you. You will always be in my prayers." He had more to say to her, but she was gone.

For a moment he stared after her, not seeing her but seeing the many kindnesses, the many times she had protected him. Why had she done it? It must be that it was God's will. And man went always as God pleased.

So now what lay before him?

Was there more torture? More ill treatment and starvation? A new cacique might have new ways to break the will of a Christian. But Juan Ortiz had survived under Ucita for three years. He had been tempered and tried. Whatever was ahead of him, he could endure. Perhaps he might yet again see the churches of Sevilla.

He hastened off holding tightly to the old man's belt.

# CHAPTER SIX

# A Brief Sweet Taste of Freedom

The path wound along the edge of swamps and through pools of water so that they ran in mud as much as on dry earth. Occasionally through the creepers and trees Juan saw the shimmering surface of the bay. But he had little time for sightseeing, for he was hard pressed to keep pace with the fast, steady trot of the ancient Floridian.

At last his guide halted on the banks of a river and said, "I leave you here, young white. I must hurry back, so as to be at Ucita by dawn. No suspicions must be cast on Acuera or on me as helpers in your escape."

Juan thanked him profusely and told him to be sure and tell Acuera how much he valued her friendship. Then, looking around, he asked, "Where is the town of Mocoço?"

"It is upstream," the other replied. "When light comes, you will be able to find the path that follows the river to the town."

Juan thanked him again, for he was grateful and aware of the danger the old man had risked in his behalf. The Indian pressed a piece of dried meat into the Spaniard's hands and was quickly gone. Juan called more thanks into the darkness after him.

For the first time since he was captured, he was alone—alone and unafraid of the sights and sounds and smells of the New World, which pressed close around him and hugged him as if he were one of its own. The water sucked in and out among the tree roots with noisy plops. Something thick and black rose in the middle of the river, swirled about, and quietly sank. Mosquitoes buzzed in his ears. Gnats crawled into his eyes. Spicy smells of fresh blossoms intermingled with the heavy odor of damp rotting leaves and mud.

The New World was no longer strange, but its familiarity had no claim on him. He was not a Floridian yet. He was still Juan Ortiz, a Spaniard from Sevilla, who yearned to see his native land again.

Turning, he felt his way downstream and came out of the trees onto the sands of the bay. It was the distant northern end of the same bay where he had gone ashore for the letter held in the split cane, the same on whose shores he had been tortured and where he had come so close to taking his own life. It was the bay where some day a ship might come to take him away, back to Spain.

He gazed out, searching all of the flat surface tilting upward to the horizon. The bay mirrored only emptiness in the light of the moon. Where was the brigantine he had once sailed on? Surely Narváez's ships would continue to search the Florida coastline for the commander and his followers and the treasure they had surely discovered. Surely one of the ships would return here to this bay where the expedition had begun.

But the pale light showed nothing, and Juan dropped to the sand and slept.

The screaming of gulls awoke him. He sat up and rubbed his eyes and sleepily watched the birds fight over a fish. A stately line of pelicans flew past. Skimmers seined the top water at the beach's edge with their red dipping bills.

The bay was still and reddish in the morning light. Far out, Indians fished from their log boat. He drew back into the bushes at sight of them. If he had to stay in Florida and be a slave, he had rather try Mocoço as master. Acuera had assured him he would be safe and kindly treated. Why should he doubt her?

He sat on a piece of driftwood, hidden from the fishing Indians, and ate his breakfast leisurely. He watched the crabs dart in and out of their holes and the many birds busy hunting food. This was freedom such as he had not enjoyed for a long time, and he was reluctant to let it go. Yet, it was dangerous to stay here where any moment he might be seized and taken back to Ucita.

With one last look across the bay, he edged back through the twisted shrubs and grass into the woods. He took the path upstream. It followed the river and was plain and broad and hard-packed from many feet.

He had not traveled far when two natives leaped from the bushes and knocked him down and began to beat him with their wooden clubs. He covered his head with his arms, shouting frantically over and over, "Mo-coço! Friend!"

At his cries they stopped and jerked him to his feet. His hands were tied behind his back. Then jabbing him with their knives, they ushered Juan along the path without a word.

# CHAPTER SEVEN

# A Christian Becomes a Savage

Juan stumbled out of the woods into bright sunlight and saw ahead of him across the savanna the scattered huts of a town. He slowed his steps, and his captors were on him at once beating him forward through the fields of maize and between the gardens and dwellings till they reached the group of houses where the cacique and his family lived. The leader was away inspecting the town granary, and one of the Indians sped off to fetch him.

The Spaniard waited, hot and tired and out of breath. Worse, his head ached from the blows of the club, a lump over his temple throbbed, and blood from a cut ran into one eye.

A few of the villagers gathered and stood staring at him with hostility. He wanted them to know he was not an enemy. "Mocoço . . . Mocoço is friend . . ." he stammered. "I am friend of Mocoço . . . Mocoço . . ."

The faces ringing him were blank, the eyes cold. Juan talked on desperately, chanting the same words again and again. Cloud shadows washed over him. No one moved or smiled.

At last a tall Indian in breechclout and moccasins approached. His face and body were tattooed. Loops of a shell necklace circled his neck, and from it a golden ornament dangled on his chest. The villagers moved back deferentially.

He stopped before Juan and inspected him intently, fanning himself all the while with a feather fan. Then he ordered the thongs cut from Juan's wrists and led the way to an open shed. A stool was brought, and the cacique sat down on it with a regal air.

"I understand you spoke my name as a friend," the cacique said. "Who are you who can say you are a friend of Mocoço? I choose my friends, not they me. I know you not. Speak!"

Juan was so relieved to have found Mocoço that he babbled about his captivity in Spanish. After a moment he realized with horror what he was doing. He calmed himself and began to tell in Timucuan about Ucita and his tortures. He showed the scars on his legs and back. He told of killing the panther.

"Acuera, the daughter of Ucita, sent me to you." Then he added hopefully, "She said you would be a kind master."

He had finished. He waited, watching the cacique's face. Mocoço gave no sign he had understood a word the Spaniard said. For the longest time he sat, the fan idle in his hand. The onlookers were still also. Juan shifted uneasily. It was difficult to wait patiently to hear what was to happen to him. Life or death?

"*Kyrie eleison*," Juan prayed. "Lord, have mercy, mercy, mercy."

The fan in Mocoço's hand once again swung back and forth before his face. The cacique smiled.

"Acuera has compassion as well as beauty," Mocoço said. "I will do as she wishes. With or without a nose, I do not care for her father. Ucita shall not have you back."

There were soft cries of delight from the onlookers. Juan glanced around at the smiling faces that now welcomed him. They seemed truly glad that he had come to them and that his life was spared. He smiled back.

Then Mocoço explained that the Spaniard would not be a slave. He would be free to go and come as he wished. If he did not run away but stayed and proved himself worthy to become a Timucuan, he would be adopted into the tribe.

Juan was startled. A member of the tribe? One of these infidel savages? Could he do such a thing? Would God forgive him for doing such a thing?

Yet, what else could he do? Till heaven sent someone to rescue him from this place, he must surely make the best of his life. These people were kind. They trusted him. He must give kindness and trust in return if he was ever again to see the shores of Spain, ever again to know the comfort of God's forgiveness.

The Spaniard bowed his head and thanked the cacique for his generosity and promised to do whatever was required of him in the best manner possible.

Standing apart from the villagers was an old man, thin and wrinkled. He had appeared to have no interest in Ortiz. Suddenly he spoke, pointing out that since all Spaniards were their enemies, it might be unwise to keep one alive among them. It must be remembered that white men were of a different nature than Timucuans and might by their very strangeness and nearness among them bring ill health or some other evil to the people of Mocoço.

The cacique nodded his head at these words. He said that the priest was wise beyond all others and that all agreed with his comments on white men. But this one seemed harmless. However, if it became apparent that this white man was evil or dangerous in any way, he would die by Mocoço's very own hands.

Mocoço turned back to Juan and added, "And while you live with us, if ever I hear of your countrymen nearby, I will send you to them so that you may again be a Spaniard and return to your own country."

Mocoço then called from the crowd a young warrior. He was shorter and more muscular than the other Timucuans. In his hand was a thick bow, and several arrows were stuck through his clubbed hair. A tall, lithe woman stood with him before the cacique.

"This is Pooy and his wife, Yua," Mocoço said. "You will live with them and learn the ways of Timucuans."

Juan was pleased, for the couple appeared to be about his own age and would not be too severe if he was slow and awkward in learning savage ways. In his soul he thanked his Lord for being merciful to him. Aloud he expressed his gratitude once more to the cacique. Then he followed the couple to their dwelling at the edge of town on the riverbank.

Pooy told his wife to prepare food for them. Leading Juan off, he showed him a bow he was making. "It shall be yours," he said. "All Timucuan men carry bows. Do not worry. I will teach you to shoot. I will help you become fine Timucuan." And he patted the Spaniard's arm.

Juan Ortiz of Sevilla a Timucuan! A Floridian! It was as wild as the most fanciful dream. He had come with Narváez to the New World to gain a fortune. Captured, tortured, and now free—he might yet find golden cities or the Fountain of Youth. The Timucuans would know of these things, if they existed.

When he was rescued, if he did not carry away great wealth, he would surely take home tales of his adventures and of the marvels and natural wonders and secrets of this New World. He would be known in Sevilla as the fireside teller of tales and have friends everywhere.

Juan listened to Pooy with a light heart. His future was as bright as the Florida sunshine.

# INTERLUDE III

America was "without form, and void," and darkness lay upon the Ocean Sea to the west of the known world.

The known world was that portion of the globe occupied by Europe, Africa, and Asia. These three interlocking continents had been assigned by God as the places for man to live. No other place existed—perhaps some living space for dragons but not for man. Theologians and philosophers and other knowing scholars all agreed on this, and they truly believed it.

During the fifteenth and sixteenth centuries Europe was overwhelmed by a number of events that shook and disturbed her inhabitants. Now we call this time a new birth, a Renaissance of culture and learning. There was a flood of enlightenment and enrichment, freedom and beauty and knowledge pouring through the world. And there was money flowing.

There was no livelier activity of the period than exploration. Ships zipped about everywhere, opening up

the darkness and letting the Renaissance sunlight in—
the sunlight of new ideas and speculations.

Sail west and reach the continent of Asia in the east
—that was one of the startling new notions. And many
people had begun to believe the world was round. One
man set out to prove the truth of the idea—Christopher
Columbus.

Columbus sailed west across the Ocean Sea and
found land. He found naked savages who shot bows
and arrows and beautiful women who wore only gold
nose plugs. And monkeys who hung by their tails.
These lands were lush and warm. Though sometimes
there were cannibals, the new-found lands were surely
the paradise all yearned to find on earth.

But could this be Asia? China? India? Then where
were the great cities and the mighty civilizations that
Marco Polo had found and told all Europe about?
They must be there. Look, search, seek everywhere.

Ships went out, spyglasses at the ready. Who would
be the one to find Cathay? Or Cipangu, rich in gold
and precious stones? Or the first to be greeted by
Asian emperors?

Amerigo Vespucci was looking. He coasted the eastern rim of South America. He saw that the lands were
not only habitable but inhabited everywhere. Was it
Asia? There were no cities, only savages and huts.
After much consideration about his explorations, he believed these new lands to the west of the known world
were a *mundus novus*—a new world!

But such a belief brought problems. Had not ancient
writers said that the Ocean Sea was uninhabited? Ren-

aissance man believed these ancients and knew their works by heart.

Yet, explorers on the western sea had found lands inhabited with as great a multitude of peoples and animals as known in Europe or Africa or Asia. They had found "much firm land and infinite islands" never mentioned by the ancient writers.

It was a problem not only for navigation and maps. Theology and philosophy and the great mass of learning handed down to Renaissance man over the ages would now have to be changed if a new world had been discovered.

The evidence was too strong. As more and more exploration went on and no sign of the Spice Islands turned up, it had to be admitted. A new world was there in the western part of the Ocean Sea. Europe would have to change the old ideas and old maps to include the new lands. But what was the shape of these lands? And what natural wonders, what curiosities, what mysteries filled them?

And here, at this very moment of history, there is no comprehensible America, not even an idea of America, of what was to come. There *is* a mysterious void land, containing only one certainty—possibilities.

There might be a fierce race of men there with the snouts of dogs. Or men who cut off captives' heads and drank their blood.

Somewhere must live the Golden Man, El Dorado, whose body was covered with gold dust. Or trumpet-blowing apes making sweet music. Or warlike Amazons with only one breast. Or knee-high men who spent their lives fighting raiding parties of long-legged storks.

Griffons and dragons must abound. There were certainly unicorns, for an explorer reported Indians wore their spiral horns as pendants. And bats as big as hawks. Sea monsters, fierce and hungry.

Mermaids might indeed sing siren songs along the coast of the New World. And unipeds—how could there be a land without these huge one-legged creatures who never needed parasols to keep away rain? For when a uniped was caught in a downpour, he lay on his back and held his big flat foot over him for protection. Europeans knew everything there was to know about unipeds. If they could only see one, they would discover it was all true. Perhaps in America . . .

And somewhere in the western sea it was said the devil lived on an island. On other isles lived square-headed Indians with bright blue mouths who roamed through the jungles eating live snakes. Who would be the first to see a one-eyed giant? Men with heads in their chests? Ants that dug up gold?

Somewhere in Florida was the Fountain of Youth. One sip and a man became young and supple and lived forever. Ponce de Leon, who had sailed west with Columbus, searched for it fruitlessly. Someday some explorer would chance upon the wonderful fountain. Or upon the Seven Cities of Cíbola. Or a tree of gold with roots tapping the globe's center.

Renaissance Europe had a great store of myths and fables and travelers' tales handed down from antiquity and from the Middle Ages. The great and the lowly knew them and accepted them as possible truth about faraway places. Just such tall tales were a part of the background of Juan Ortiz. Whatever his feelings about living with the Indians in Florida, in some part of his mind he might have welcomed the chance to be the first to see one of these wonders, the first to step into the misty wilderness of fantasy.

# CHAPTER EIGHT

# The Broken Cross

The town was much like that of Ucita, with thatched houses scattered around the open square. Where Ucita lived on top of a mound, Mocoço had a house partly submerged in the ground for summer coolness. The rest of the year the cacique moved about among his several dwellings.

There was a mound in the town, housing a temple with a carved wooden rooster on its roof. The priest who had spoken out against Juan performed ceremonies here.

Since Juan could not be a Timucuan hunter and warrior without knowing how to shoot a bow and arrow, he wanted to begin learning at once. But Pooy pointed out that first he needed a dwelling place. The two set to work felling palmetto trees with a stone ax. These trunks were then split and laid flat side up on a scaffold waist-high above the ground. The roof was covered with bundles of palmetto leaves. There were no sides to the house, but flexible cane mats could be used if needed.

Juan often laughed to see his home, for it was little more than a covered platform. It would never do as a dwelling in Spain, but for Florida it was ideal. Should the river overflow its banks, he would be dry above the swirling waters. The thatch roof kept off rain and the fierce rays of the sun. With no sides, breezes could reach him in hot weather. And if anything destroyed the house, another could be built with little effort—as there was never a lack of materials.

It was just like Pooy's, only smaller. Juan slept on a pile of moss collected from the trees. His few possessions hung from the roof rafters. Yua gave him a section of a small tree trunk to use as a pillow.

Pooy and Juan did not work on the house every day. Some days Pooy chose not to work but to lie around at ease. And some days he took time off to hunt. On those days Juan helped Yua gather roots and herbs, or he cut firewood or fished in the river beside his dwelling.

By the time the dwelling was finished to Pooy's satisfaction, the fall winds and rains were upon them. Many of the town families wandered through the woods at this season gathering acorns and other nuts, grapes and persimmons. Pooy and Yua with Juan left the village, too, carrying only a clay pot, a drill for starting fires, and weapons.

It was a life such as only traveling gypsies lived in Spain, but to Juan it was a source of delight and wonder. Every night found them sleeping at a different site, unless the weather was bad. Then families might stay together in one place for days, singing and playing cane flutes and telling stories. Always they shared their food with each other, and always they included Juan in their activities.

When the sun broke through the overcast, the families separated. Some headed for the coast to eat oysters and crabs roasted in hot ashes. Others stayed in the pine woods, eating lizards and snakes and small game, sleeping on the thick mat of needles with the trees soughing soothingly overhead.

Once Juan and Pooy and Yua crouched among the tall grasses of a savanna as the swirling purple clouds of a hurricane swept across the land. They whistled at the winds to make them go away, for that was the Timucuan custom. Juan whistled till his throat was dry and his lips cramped, but mostly he tried to remember prayers to save them.

The days warmed and the woods and meadows were sweet-scented with spring blossoms. Alligators roared in their water holes. Herons took over whole woods for their treetop rookeries. Once more the skies were bright and cloudless blue.

The three wanderers returned to the village to plant their fields of maize and the vegetable gardens. Juan wanted to help with the work, but Pooy would not allow it. He must learn to handle a bow or else he would be a Spaniard forever and Mocoço would not like that.

Every morning Juan went to the river meadow behind his dwelling. He set up a target of bark against a sandy hummock and shot arrows at it from various angles and distances. Sometimes a village boy joined him in practice and teased Juan about his frequent misses.

Juan did not mind, nor did it bother him that his bow was a small one such as all the young Timucuans began shooting with. In time he would have the skill and strength to use the long powerful bows of the warriors. At least he hoped he would.

The townspeople beached their dugouts on the bank near where Juan practiced. As they passed to and from their boats, many called out encouragement, others friendly ridicule. The Timucuans were especially amused when Juan not only missed the target but also the small hill behind it. Then they laughed uproariously.

Whenever a group of boats floated past the meadow headed for the sea, Juan asked them to look for a great ship with sails and to be sure and come back and tell Mocoço and him about it. Spanish colonists and explorers were everywhere in the New World. Ships plied back and forth all the time. Surely they sailed often up and down the coast of Florida. Surely one would rescue him.

Fishing group after group returned and shouted out cheerfully to Juan that no great ships had been seen by them. He no longer suffered from the strangling fear and despair of his first days and nights as a captive. Still he longed for home at times. Still he felt a stranger, alone, alien, among the Indians. And sometimes he wondered—would help never come?

He did not show his feelings. Besides, there was too much to do to dwell on them long. Food had to be gotten, arrows and knives made, and household services performed. The round of daily and seasonal tasks went steadily on, and Juan was so involved in them that he had no time for sad spirits.

One day when Juan was walking across the square, he saw several warriors talking to the temple priest. He stopped to listen. They had just returned from fishing in the bay, and one of them was telling that he had found the remains of a white man washed ashore. The clothes were gone and most of the flesh had been eaten by sea creatures, but one shiny ornament remained around the man's neck. The fisherman held out his open fist.

Juan moved closer to see. There in the palm lay a silver cross and a chain. The blessed Holy Cross! Tears welled up in his eyes, and before he could stop himself, he snatched it from the Timucuan and kissed it.

The warrior grabbed Juan's arm and held it in a fierce grasp. Then Juan realized with horror how rude he had been. Timucuans did not snatch objects from each other or handle possessions without permission from the owner. He had offended the Indian.

Quickly Juan returned the cross and offered to trade for it. The Indian said nothing.

Juan had very few possessions, but he was willing to give all he had—two long pieces of flint he had intended shaping into knives; sinews for bow strings; bundles of colored feathers; and a strange shiny stone found in the stomach of a sea bird.

The warrior hesitated, and Juan remembered he had an otter skin and added that. Smiling, the Indian agreed and handed Juan the cross. Both arms were broken, and only tiny stubs were left. But Juan kissed it reverently once again and with trembling fingers slipped the chain over his neck and let the cross dangle on his chest. It flashed in the sun, a cross of fire. Here in this pagan land Juan now had an emblem of Christianity to sustain him.

Juan glanced up and was startled. He had forgotten the others were there. Now they ringed him, watching what a strange creature the white man was. What had made him act this way? Juan read the questions in their eyes. He looked from one to another as they stared hostilely. Among them was the temple priest, and his gaze forebode no good.

# CHAPTER NINE

# A Strange Plague

That autumn was a dangerous one for Juan. It might certainly have been his last autumn but for the staunch friendship of Mocoço.

Ucita had finally learned Juan's whereabouts, and he sent several messengers to ask for his slave's return. Each time Mocoço refused, saying that a slave so odious to Ucita was a small loss indeed. Then Ucita made friends with Mocoço's brother-in-law and sent him to fetch the Spaniard.

Juan feared for his life when he saw the brother-in-law enter the village with his armed warriors. His captivity had now become a family quarrel among the caciques, and in such a situation the white man would surely be the one to suffer. Yet, the occasion passed without incident. Mocoço feted and entertained his brother-in-law and his followers for a few days, then sent them back empty-handed.

Juan told the cacique how grateful he was. Mocoço dismissed his generosity lightly, saying that neither Ucita nor his own brother-in-law were friends of his.

And even with combined forces they were not strong enough to wage warfare with him and the many towns under him. He assured Juan that he was held in high esteem and that he was becoming a fine Timucuan.

That was good to hear, and with relief Juan settled back into his easy-going ways with Pooy and Yua.

Every day Yua rubbed her husband's skin with oil, and now she included Juan, too. Since all he wore was a breechclout, the oil protected his exposed skin from the sun's rays and the drying winds. Also it discouraged the ever present gnats and mosquitoes.

Yua helped Juan bundle his long hair together at the back of his head, so that he could carry arrows stuck in the strands as all Timucuan warriors did. Now the Spaniard was hardly distinguishable from the village warriors.

The Indians ate any time they were hungry, quite often getting up in the middle of the night to stuff themselves. So Yua kept a pot of something over the low fire beside her dwelling all the time—meat stewed with melons, or fish seasoned with herbs, or bread warmed in the hot ashes.

Whenever rainy days kept the three inside, they sat together cross-legged on the floor and talked. Pooy would tell of visiting Mocoço's other towns as one of his guards and of raids against their enemies, the Calusa Indians to the south. Yua instructed Juan in taboos and superstitions. Never cry when a woodpecker is making a noise, for then you will have a nosebleed. Do not eat the first corn gathered in a newly cultivated field. Let the temple priest bless a new fishweir.

There were hundreds of things to do or not to do. Juan despaired that he would ever learn them all so that he would be a proper Timucuan and not have evil befall him. But he noticed that Pooy did not always take the superstitions too seriously, ignoring them when they hindered what he was doing. It made Juan feel easier about his own failures.

Yua was tattooed in a strange blue and black design on her right shoulder and down around her breast on that side. She explained she had this done just after she and Pooy were married. The man who did the work demanded many gifts for his services. This much tattooing was all she and Pooy could afford, but later she would have more done. Pooy said he would begin tattoos on his body as his exploits in war and hunting became greater. Only the cacique and the most renowned warriors were heavily tattooed.

Sometimes Juan told his friends of Spain and of wheeled carriages and the splendors of the churches. He explained the significance of the cross he wore about his neck and what a great comfort it was to him here far from his home and church.

These happy talks and their days of constant companionship ended that autumn. In the weeks of falling leaves many of the villagers became sick, and few families went wandering as was their custom. They stayed at home and waited for the priest to cure them of their ailments.

The hurricane season was over, yet strong winds continued, springing up suddenly and with a great roar descending on the town, hurling tree branches, dead birds, and sand through the streets. Dark purple clouds hung low and threatening, and the sun was not seen sometimes for days and days. At nights the sky glowed with strange dancing fires.

One morning Yua did not get up. She was feverish and refused to eat. She became delirious, and Pooy had to hold her on her bed. Juan offered to help in any way he could. But Pooy told him to go away, that he was the cause of Yua's sickness and that of the other Timucuans also.

This shocked Juan. How could he possibly cause the sickness? Pooy must have made the accusation because he was upset at his wife's illness. Yet when Juan walked about the town, the streets at once emptied. No Timucuan stayed to call out greetings or ask politely about his marksmanship as they formerly had. He had changed into a stranger once again, slipped back into the skin of a distrusted and hated Spaniard. Pooy was right. The sickness and the deaths it caused were being blamed on him.

Perhaps they would kill him. Should he escape now while no one guarded him? He could take the path through the woods to the bay. That would be easy to follow. Yet, he dared not leave and take the risk of capture by Ucita or his friends. He could only stay and place his hopes in Mocoço. Surely the cacique would not let Juan be killed on account of this mysterious sickness. Surely the plague would pass soon, and he and the Timucuans would be friends and neighbors again.

Now his days were spent getting food and cooking

it. With his bow he hunted small game on the savannas
and in the marshes close to the village. He feared to go
too far away lest he become lost. His meals were
mostly fish caught in the cane trap Yua had made for
him. When it failed, he fished in the river back of his
house with cane pole and line.

One day Juan sat inside his dwelling listening to the
wild cries of Yua as she thrashed about in pain. It
upset him to hear her suffering and not be able to help
her. He couldn't see her, for Pooy had hung woven
reed mats around the sides of the building.

After a while she quieted and Pooy came outside.
Juan called out a greeting and asked about Yua. The
Timucuan did not answer. He stood before his house
for a long time, his arms limp at his sides and his head
bowed. Then he roused himself and, turning, came
slowly toward Juan.

"The priest wants to kill you," Pooy said softly,
standing before the Spaniard, but not looking at him,
"for you are the cause of all the sickness. You and the
god you wear about your neck."

Juan sat up, alarmed and tense.

"The Timucuan gods are jealous of your god," Pooy
went on. "That is what the temple priest says, and he
would destroy you and your shining god in order to
break the spell of evil on our town."

Juan saw once more the fires and the *barbacoa* of
Ucita and smelled again his own burning flesh. Was it
all to happen again?

"In time the temple priest will have his way," Pooy

told him. "For now, Mocoço will not let him harm you, saying that you are good, that the evil comes from elsewhere. Mocoço says the god you wear is only an ornament, just as we wear stone or shell pendants. But if the sickness lasts and more die, the priest will have his way."

Now Pooy looked at Juan and said, "I want to ask a favor of you. I know how much you respect your god, for you carry it everywhere with you, night and day. But will you give it to me to take to the priest? He believes he can kill your god. Perhaps that will help Yua and the others."

He looked away across the river where a white heron sailed. "Yua begged me not to ask you this favor, for it was not a right thing to ask. But I must. Yua has been sick too long."

Juan's hand went to the cross. Kill his God? No one could kill his God. He would never let the priest have the cross.

It was curious. The cross had not been in his thoughts very much since it had come to him. He had meant to hold it while he said his prayers every day. But there was so much to do. The words were hard to remember. Spanish words, Latin words, they sounded strange to him now. Perhaps it was true. He only wore it now as Pooy wore his conch-shell necklace, because he was used to it, because he liked it. It was not really his God.

His fingers found the little stumps of arms. It was already broken. Suddenly it did not seem to him so important a thing. Perhaps it had been sent to save his life again, as once Acuera had done. And at last he slipped the chain over his head.

"Take it," he said to Pooy. "If it will help Yua, I am glad."

Later he was afraid. The strange weather went on, Yua still lay moaning on her pallet, and the sickness still struck now here, now there. Then one day Yua sat up in her skin bed and asked for water. She was thin and yellow but seemed brighter and better. In a few days she was well on her way to full recovery. No one else fell ill.

The days became sunny, the breezes warm and fragrant. Blossoms opened among the round lily pads floating on the swamps. The savanna turned a fresh green overnight. And birds, large and small, plain and brilliantly colored, were everywhere singing their songs.

Wall mats were rolled up and the houses again open and airy. The Timucuans were up and bustling about again. Juan Ortiz fished and hunted and played gambling games with his friends. Around his neck hung a curiously shaped stone with a hole in it, which Pooy had found on the beach.

# INTERLUDE IV

In Florida food was plentiful, the weather warm, and the living easy. And yet the Timucuans needed a great deal of help in their daily struggles against the forces of nature and the unseen powers that threatened them.

A Frenchman wrote, "They have their priests, to whom they give great credit, because they are great magicians, great soothsayers, and callers upon the devils. These priests serve them instead of physicians and surgeons; they carry always about with them a bag full of herbs and drugs, to cure the sick . . ."

A Spanish priest lumped all these practitioners together under the name of "sorcerers," while others labeled them "jugglers" and "divinators" and "conjurors."

No matter what the early European visitors chose to call those engaged in magic and medicine and religion, their power had to be acknowledged. They ranked in importance next to the cacique, and no activity took place without their presence.

Before a field was tilled, the priest offered a prayer to make the crop grow abundantly. When the first corn was gathered by the tribe, he was there to perform the proper ceremonies; he blessed the corncrib where the ears were stored; and he executed other rituals when the first flour was made from the grains.

A newly made fishweir might prove useless unless the priest said certain words and phrases over it. Parties of warriors dared not hunt game without letting the priest consecrate all their arrows. And if the first arrow missed, the priest had then to begin his ceremonies all over to make sure the second one brought down the game.

The earliest record of aboriginal weather control in eastern America was noted among the Timucuans. Certain priests had the power to hold back the rain in threatening thunderclouds by blowing toward the sky and chanting various formulas. On the other hand, there were specialists who knew how to bring water down from the clouds when it was needed for the crops.

For his services the priest was paid in pearls, paint, ornaments, food, ambergris, or whatever those he assisted had at hand. But surely no work was as profitable as that of doctoring, for the European chroniclers noted that there were many sharp practices for extorting fees.

Even if the pay demanded for a cure was met, the man of medicine might keep the patient suffering till more was given. Or he could let the sick Timucuan recover, then injure him through some form of witchcraft so that treatment had to begin all over again and another fee could be collected.

It was reported that the medicine man had the power to keep a child from being born and would do so unless the parents satisfied his greedy demands. Sometimes the priest declared that a terrible disease or a great calamity was about to destroy the whole town. Then he assured the perplexed and trembling inhabitants that he, and only he, knew how to avert the danger, but that it would take piles and piles of gifts for him to bring forth all his powerful magic and concentrate it against the threatening disaster.

Though the priest of medicine schemed for illegal gain, there was a certain amount of risk involved in his work. His methods of curing might fail and his own incantations and magic turn against him and kill him, or cause him much pain and a great deal of trouble before he could cure himself.

Then, too, a Timucuan who continued on his sick bed for a long period might become suspicious of his medicine man and hire some other priest to burn down his doctor's hut or use witchcraft to harm or kill him. This was a fine way for one man of medicine to get rid of a rival, and such shenanigans among these priests must have provided a great deal of entertainment for the Timucuans not directly involved.

A priest who adhered simply to leading religious rites had an easier and less dangerous existence than one who practiced medicine. However, this may not have always been true since very little was reported by the chroniclers on Timucuan religious beliefs other than that the tribe revered the sun and moon. Perhaps the Timucuans were not very religious. Once, though, they were filled with enough pious zest to add a new god to their pantheon—a unique god represented by an idol.

The idol was a stone pillar on which were the arms of the king of France. This had been erected when French explorers first landed on the east coast of Florida in 1562 to denote their country's ownership. Two years later when French colonists arrived, they found the column decorated with a crown of bay leaves and garlands of flowers. Before it were offerings of fruits, vegetables, and edible roots; gourd vessels of oil; a quiver of arrows and a bow.

They were amazed to see the Timucuans kneel before this stone pillar and worship it and kiss it reverently. The Indians invited the French Huguenots to share their god with them and to kiss it as they did.

The artist, Jacques le Moyne, had been sent with the colonists to map the New World and to portray the Florida natives and their customs. He was much impressed by the religious ritual the Timucuans had evolved in the two years since the column had been erected, and he painted a picture of the ceremony.

Of his many paintings of the episodes of the Huguenot colony and its Timucuan neighbors, this is the only original that has survived. It shows the bedecked column with the heraldic arms of the French king, the kneeling Indians, and a wonderful assortment of offerings. To one side stands the tall and handsome cacique, tattooed in red and blue designs and talking to the shorter French leader dressed in a yellow suit with blue stockings and a fancy satin hat. Behind the leader are soldiers in metal helmets and pink candy-striped breeches.

It is a handsome painting and most realistic. However, the complexion of the natives is puzzling, for they are all tinted a strange pale pink. American Indians? Perhaps their bodies were smeared with white clay or ground-up chalky shell. It might be that Le Moyne was merely using artistic license for the best possible results. After all, were not savages with glowing pink skins, looking for all the world as if they had just stepped forth from a fragrant bubble bath, more striking than the usual coppery oily natives?

It seems odd that no priest was depicted, odd because the priest was involved in every aspect of Timucuan life. No doubt the picture's balance left no place for him, but undoubtedly one was close by when the pillar idol was being worshiped.

Were they frauds, these priests, shamans, magicians, and others? The early European chroniclers considered them that, but the Timucuans and their neighbors of southeastern America certainly did not. They believed in their tricks of legerdemain, ventriloquism, and hypnosis, and in their power to deal with spirits through chants, sacred formulas and herbs, as well as by fits and hallucinations. And a great deal of showmanship at all times helped to buttress the people's faith.

It wasn't only the patients who believed in the priest of magic and medicine and religion, for it was said the priest himself believed explicitly in his own efficiency and took his cures seriously—so seriously, in fact, that when he was in pain and suffering, he placed himself in the hands of a fellow practitioner to be cured. And that is certainly the finest testimonial.

# CHAPTER TEN

# Sneak Attack

Yua could not find enough work to do. Juan had never known her to be idle, but since she had recovered from her sickness, she bustled about more industriously than ever. She scolded Pooy and Juan for not shooting more birds. She wanted their feathers for a cloak she was making for herself. She skinned game, cleaned and smoked more eels and fish than they needed, wove innumerable baskets, and gathered enough roots to feed them for a long time.

Pooy watched her in amazement. "She must have swallowed a whirlwind," he told the Spaniard, "and that is what makes her rush about like this."

One day Mocoço sent Pooy and several of his other attendants to the sea to kill manatees. They were to bring back the flesh for a feast the cacique planned. Pooy told Juan that Mocoço also wanted certain bones found in the manatee's head. These he would use in a religious ceremony.

The warriors assembled at the town's boat landing, and a priest was there to bless their venture and give prayers for successful fishing. As they piled into the dugouts, Juan called out, "Pooy, do not forget to watch carefully for a Spanish ship."

He never gave up hope of rescue and always reminded those going to the sea of Mocoço's promise. Though the Timucuans often told him they did not want him to leave them and would never tell him of sighting a ship so he would have to stay, Juan knew they were teasing. They would not lie if they saw his countrymen hereabouts.

Pooy promised he would watch day and night. The others shouted that it was well known that Pooy had such poor eyesight he could not see even his toes but that they would do the looking for Juan.

When the fishermen finally returned, Pooy reported no Spanish ships. But they had sighted and killed many manatees. And Pooy had brought back shark teeth and a bag of conch shells.

Yua had never mentioned the cross that Juan had given to the priest, but now she set to work to replace it. She bored holes in the shark teeth and strung them on a piece of deer sinew for Juan to wear. She took the conches and broke off the outer shell. By cutting and sanding these pieces, she shaped them into various designs to wear as pendants.

The hard center core of the conch was spiraled and looked much like the whorled horn of a unicorn. Juan had seen Timucuans wearing these on thongs and had been fooled into believing them unicorn horns. However, he had never seen the animal in Florida, and when he described it to Pooy, the Indian said it did not live there. So now Juan knew.

Yua took the spiral columns and cut them into small beads. With a thin sliver of flint she bored a hole in each one and then strung them all into a necklace. Some of the cores she made into ear pins.

Pooy pierced Juan's ear lobes so he could wear the shell pins and also fish bladders dyed red. These bladders were inserted in the earlobes, then blown up and tied so that they stayed inflated. They were most handsome ornaments, for they shone red as rare carbuncle stones.

In late winter it was the custom of the Timucuans to take to the town square a large stag skin with the skull and antlers attached. There the women stuffed the skin with the roots the villagers used as food. Garlands of flowers and leaves were hung around the deer's neck, along with strings of various fruits.

Then while a band of musicians played on their cane flageolets, the stuffed animal was placed in the fork of a dead tree at the edge of the square. Mocoço and the temple priest stood below the deer, offering prayers to the sun to make the crops grow, and the villagers behind them chanted and sang.

The deer was left in the tree after the ceremony and no more notice taken of it. The birds picked it to pieces and knocked the antlers to the ground, but no one cared.

Sometimes hunters stalking a herd of deer used deerskins as a disguise. The skin covered the Indian's body and his bow and arrows. The skull fitted over his head like a mask, and he was able to see out of the deer's eye sockets. Creeping through the grass, the stalker could often get very close to grazing deer without arousing their suspicions.

Pooy and Juan often hunted in this way. Pooy could tell by the jerk of a deer's head or its snort or the way it stamped its feet whether it was communicating with those around it or getting ready to bolt. Juan did not yet have this knowledge, but he still managed to shoot a great deal of game by stalking.

At times he and Pooy hunted with a large group of the town men. The priest blessed all the arrows they were taking with them and chanted rituals as he danced around a fire of burning tobacco. As payment for performing this sacred rite, the priest received the first deer killed.

Across the river from Juan's dwelling was a wide savanna. At the far end were scattered ponds and marshes where birds of all kinds gathered. Spoonbills and ibises walked the muddy edges of the pools, feeding on small fishes and snails. Snakebirds sank in the dark marsh water until only their heads and black skinny necks showed. Gallinules jogged through the stiff grasses on green feet. Rails, coots, and herons were all around, diving for food among lily pads, stalking through the reeds, or floating asleep on the open water.

Pooy and Juan hunted here whenever Yua wanted colored feathers for a cloak or a fan or for trading. Sometimes Juan came to the pools to be by himself. He had a favorite spot where a half-fallen live oak leaned

out over the water. Here he sat in a crotch, high
enough to see out over the marshlands and ponds. Hidden by sheets of moss, he watched all that happened
among the inhabitants of this wet world.

It was a lovely place, peaceful and green and
strange. Sometimes sitting there, he happened to think
of his home in Spain. How different that seemed—and
far away and in its way as strange as this big moss-cov-
ered tree and the bird-filled ponds.

One day he was sitting in this hidden spot. The wind
rippled the water in odd crinkly designs and sent coots
rocking wildly among the lily pads and grass stalks.
The breeze died away and fat clouds appeared on the
calm waters, and their dark shapes slid across the
smooth sea of grass.

Out on the savanna something moved among the
still grass. Juan followed the bending and swaying
sedge curiously. Was it a herd of deer passing or villagers returning from a hunt? He could not tell. Then
where the grass was thin he saw a file of armed,
painted warriors skulking toward the village. They
were not Timucuans.

He slid quickly down the oak trunk and, picking up
his bow and arrows, raced off. He heard the cries of
the attackers. He sprinted harder and at last reached
the river and splashed across.

Smoke from blazing huts filled the streets, and people dashed in confusion from one end of the village to
the other. Women guided and pushed crying children
up the slope into the temple on the mound. Men flew
about firing arrows and answering the war cries of the

enemy with shrieks of their own. Around Mocoço's dwelling Timucuans fought the invaders hand-to-hand with clubs and knives.

Juan turned toward Pooy's house to see if he and Yua were safe. Pooy would tell him what to do to help. Then he saw behind the house a painted warrior sneaking through the bushes with the decapitated head of a Timucuan woman.

Juan slipped behind a tree and notched an arrow to his bow string. The enemy paused and glanced around to see if he was being pursued. Seeing no one, he stood and leaped down the riverbank. Juan stepped from behind the tree and drew the arrow back. Aiming quickly, he released it. The arrow sank in the warrior's back up to its feathered end. He screamed and threw out an arm as he sprawled forward down the mud slope. The head rolled before him into the shallow water.

"That was a fine shot," called Pooy, running toward him from the direction of the town. "I have been looking for you. I was afraid the Calusa might have captured you."

The Calusa were a tribe living to the south of the territory of the Timucuans, and the two groups had always been on unfriendly terms.

"I saw the war party crossing the savanna and followed," Juan told him, "and arrived just in time to see this one slipping away."

Pooy took the severed head from the river and held it gently, with sadness in his eyes. It was the wife of a kinsman of Yua's. He must take it to the family so proper mourning ceremonies could begin.

He took a cane knife from his belt and cut to the bone around the top of the head of the slain Calusan. Loosening the scalp with his fingers, he jerked it off and handed it to Juan.

"Go dry the scalp over the fire," Pooy said. "I will come back and cut off his limbs later." He walked off, and there was nothing for Juan to do but what he had been told. He made his way to his dwelling with the bloody scalp at arm's length before him.

# CHAPTER ELEVEN

# War Against the Calusans

Vultures found the bodies of two Calusans, who had crawled off to die in the tall grass beyond the village. Pooy said it was unusual for the slain to be left behind by any raiding party. Men killed in battle were usually fetched back to their homes and buried with great pomp and reverence.

Pooy said his people had fought so fiercely that the Calusans did not have time to search for their comrades' bodies. Now their scalps and limbs would be added to the trophies taken from the warrior Juan had killed, to be stuck on spears, decorated with branches of laurel, and exhibited in the square.

"Three enemy dead is a victory," Pooy added. "But there is no time for a celebration. Mocoço has ordered the town to prepare at once for a retaliation raid."

"Our cacique is smart," Yua added proudly. "He knows the Calusans won't expect us so soon after their raid. We will take them unawares and have a great victory. Then we will celebrate."

Juan said nothing, but it did not seem much of a victory. Several Timucuans were wounded so severely that they were dying. Also, a number of women and children had been taken away as slaves, not to mention the many burned huts. He shrugged. What did one Spaniard know about it?

Yua was grateful to Juan for saving the head of her kinswoman. It meant a great deal to the family that the head could be buried with her body. Now the woman's ghost would not go roaming about making trouble but lie quiet among the Indians. Yua thanked Juan again and again and praised his skill with the bow.

A few days after the raid, Mocoço summoned the Spaniard to him. He was strolling with his youngest wife. She was not as pretty as Acuera, but then a cacique usually married for political reasons, not for love and beauty. Mocoço doubtless would never add Acuera to his train of wives, after all, for her father did not have great power or many villages under his control. Mocoço hated Ucita, and Ucita returned the feeling. Still if it had proved expedient, the two might have worked something out.

Mocoço invited Juan to accompany them among the trees and farms behind his dwelling houses. The cacique and his advisers often walked here when discussing important matters. Juan found it cool and pleasant to stroll along the walkways. The breeze had blown away the swarms of biting flies usually present at this time.

Overhead, tiny colored birds drifted through the streamers of moss, while parrakeets squawked and clowned along branches. Lizards scuttled across the paths or sat watchful and unblinking on stones. A dragonfly paused in midair to whir its wings and stare into Juan's face.

The three stopped at a pool, a dammed-up part of the stream that flowed into the nearby river. A tall pink flamingo stood at one side, its neck twisted about as it scratched its back with its awkward-looking beak.

Mocoço clucked softly to it, and the bird wobbled toward him on its thin stilt legs. He handed his wife a bag, from which she took small snails to feed the bird. One snail after another disappeared from the woman's hand till the bag was empty.

Then they moved on to a herbal garden tended by two old women. Mocoço plucked various aromatic leaves and crushed them in his fingers for the Spaniard to sniff, telling him the name of the plant and its use.

One plant with a small undistinguished flower had sticky leaves. The cacique caught a golden beetle and dropped it onto one of the leaves. At once the hairs along the leaf's edges curled over the beetle to hold it tight, like so many human fingers. Mocoço said the beetle would be eaten by the plant.

"I want a big plant just like this," he told Juan. "One I can feed my enemies to." He did not smile as he said this.

They began to walk again, and Mocoço complimented Juan on his alertness in shooting the fleeing Calusan. "Pooy tells me you are very good with the bow," he said.

"I have learned to shoot it—that is all that Pooy

should say," Juan replied modestly. In truth, all the villagers knew he was not expert.

"Pooy reports to me on your progress with our customs and skills," Mocoço went on. "Praise is all I ever
hear from his lips."

"Pooy and Yua are much too generous and kind,"
Juan answered. "I fear I am a slow pupil, but I appreciate their patience with me. And yours also."

Mocoço waved his hand in a generous gesture. "You
are becoming a fine Timucuan—yet—" He paused. "Yet
I cannot take you with me on the raid on the Calusans."

Juan had not expected to go. He did not mind staying in the village and guarding the women and children when the warriors left.

"There are a great many ceremonies to go through
with," Mocoço explained. "Many things to do and even
more *not* to do. Any taboo broken, even accidently,
and my war party would have to turn back and begin
the ceremonies all over again."

He placed his hand on the Spaniard's shoulder and
smiled at him. "We place ourselves in the war priest's
hands, and he does not want you to go," Mocoço said.
"You might make one wrong move and bring bad luck
to us. It is not that I do not trust you . . . but . . . that
the priest wishes it thus."

Juan nodded cheerfully. It was all right with him.
He did not have enough training to be a Timucuan
warrior and battle their long-time enemy, the Calusans. Warfare, Indian or white, was not something he

would ever excel in. He had come on the Narváez expedition, not as a soldier, but as a laborer. After all, he had worked at many different tasks in Sevilla since early childhood.

"After my return," Mocoço went on, "I will see about your adoption into the tribe."

For the next few days the town bustled with activity day and night. It was a happy time, and there was much singing and joking among the people. Food was taken from the storehouses and specially prepared for the war party. Weapons were inspected, plans made for the travel route and for the attack.

Juan made arrows till his dwelling floor was covered with them. He was good at the work and quick, and he made them for Pooy and his friends. Pooy put a new sinew string on his bow, but he spent most of his time inserting a long, sharp antler point into his war club.

When the work was finished, he showed Yua and Juan how he was going to fight with it. He hid in the bushes, then crept up close to Juan's house with the club in his hand. Suddenly he leaped up and commenced to swing the club this way and that. He prodded and hacked with it, dodging blows from his imaginary enemy all the while.

Juan almost laughed to see how serious his friend was, how he worked himself into a rage of hate so that his eyes flashed and his voice trembled. Yua admired her husband's dance and shouted encouragement to him. She nudged Juan fiercely when she wanted him to notice some especially fine caper.

At last with a mighty swing and a triumphant whoop, Pooy slew his combatant. When he turned toward them, Juan said, "I would certainly fear to meet you in battle."

"Yes," agreed Yua with proud affection, "he is fierce! So very fierce!"

Pooy handed his club to Juan. "Here, swing it yourself. It is just right. I will kill many Calusans with it."

Juan did not perform a battle dance with it, though his friends encouraged him to. But he did swing the club about and found it nicely balanced. However, it was too heavy for him to use with any ease. Pooy waved it about as if it had the weight of only a feather.

At last all was ready. The war party bathed in water steeped with various herbs. Then the town assembled on the square, where the warriors circled Mocoço. Water in two wooden platters was brought to the cacique, and a fire was lighted before him.

Suddenly Mocoço uttered strange deep sounds and jumped about and rolled his eyes. The warriors repeated the yells and rattled their weapons. After a while they quieted, and the fighters squatted.

Now Mocoço picked up a platter of water and held it up toward the sun, praying to the day star for victory. "As I scatter this water," he thundered, "so may the enemy's blood be scattered."

With that he threw the water into the air so that it fell on his warriors. "As I have done with this water," he intoned, "so I pray that you do to the blood of your enemies."

Then he poured the water from the other vessel onto the fire, calling out, "So may you extinguish the Calusans and return with their scalps."

The people parted, and Mocoço led his fighters off through the village toward the south. The Timucuans cheered and shouted till the war party was out of sight.

# INTERLUDE V

War—war made Timucuan life worth living.

One lived by farming and hunting and fishing. It was inevitable. It had to be. But warfare made that life worth the effort.

War was a diversion from the daily and seasonal routines of village and tribal life. Warfare was drama and entertainment. Warfare was adventure. It was the way to fame and rank among the Indians. And it was intertwined with their religion.

There were rituals to go through in preparation for warfare and rituals to follow on the return from the fighting. Silly rules and customs they may appear to us, but no more silly than the rituals and folderol of chivalry of the European Middle Ages. Was not chivalry also a road to glory and a way to have fun, games, and excitement?

The Timucuans, as well as the other tribes in southeastern America, waged war to run risks and to kill an enemy. They did not try to gain more land, or to subjugate another tribe, or even to drive the enemy from his own territory. There was no objective, and there was no need to spoil the fun and the games of warfare by winning.

Victory meant the end of war. And that would never do. War was the "beloved occupation"; a necessity. Even games were preliminaries to the real thing and therefore called "the little brother of war."

Not only did the individual Indian need warfare, but the aboriginal tribe needed it also. A cacique had a difficult time holding his followers together. He could use force or fear. But what was better was a common cause to create internal unity. The tribe that stayed together survived. A headman knew that.

So the cacique considered warfare a great blessing for all concerned, for by external strife he could achieve internal tribal harmony. All the plans for a raid on an enemy, all the rites and ceremonies that must be performed, the making and the checking of weapons—all this kept the people working together and happy.

War—it was a luxury that not every tribe could afford. There had to be plenty of food. A warrior required a nourishing diet to be in tip-top fighting shape. Sugar and starch from fruits, grains, and roots; protein and fat from game and fish.

The Timucuans had all this variety.

Also, there had to be adequate food supplies gathered and stored. Warfare took men away from their share of the work in getting food. Prolonged warfare could starve a village.

The Timucuans had public granaries built of earth and thickly roofed with palm leaves, cool, dry places where were stored supplies available to the villagers at any time.

Besides food, materials for weapons were needed, and again there was no problem for the Timucuans.

A wide variety of trees in the hardwood forests of Florida furnished wood for bows. One chronicler mentions bows made from oak; another says they were of a wood darker than yew. This might mean black locust, a tough, springy wood much used among southeastern tribes. Though tribal customs might have been followed in selecting only certain kinds of bow wood, it was more likely that an individual made his weapon of whatever suited him.

A Spaniard wrote: "The bows are of the same height as he who carries them, and as the Indians of La Florida are generally of tall stature, their bows are more than two varas in length and thick in proportion." A vara equals 2.78 feet, so that makes the Florida bow about the same length as the famous British longbow.

Bowstrings were made from the sinews of deer or other large animals. The sinews were softened in water, torn apart, and then several twisted together to make a stout cord. Squirrel skin could be used but was not as good as the sinews. Another kind was made from the thick skin on the deer's neck. The string was cut from the skin spirally, then twisted for greater strength. Bear gut was also used at times.

The bows were powerful, and the string sprang forward with great force at the arrow's release. To keep the left arm from injury by the string, a wrist guard of feathers or of leather was worn.

Most chroniclers agree that usually the Floridians' arrows were made of reed, i.e., cane, which grew in great abundance along the streams and marshes. These cane arrows were tipped with almost any sharp-pointed object at hand: deer antlers, snake teeth, fish bones and scales, spurs of the turkey cock, flint stones, or even barbed wood. Feathers were glued to the notched end with a glue made from deer horns boiled to a jelly.

The Timucuans carried arrows stuck in their hair bundled at the back of their heads. They also had quivers made of deerskin in which could be carried a large number of arrows to supplement the few in their hair.

Bows and arrows were used for long or short range: in an ambush, as retreat protection, and for setting fire to houses. For close fighting the Timucuans had wooden clubs. These were shaped generally like baseball bats, though shorter and thicker. They might have fishbones or other sharp objects set into the wood to inflict greater damage, or even a whole row of such objects.

The Indians of Florida had knives of cane, shell, and stone, and also spears with short shafts. These were not considered weapons for warfare but were for hunting.

The French on the east coast of Florida said they never observed regular battle among the Timucuans, that all their military operations were either secret forays or light skirmishes, with fresh men constantly replacing the fighters. The side that killed the first enemy claimed the victory, no matter how many warriors they later lost in the skirmish.

They also told of a Timucuan chief who before a skirmish summoned to him a sorcerer who was one hundred and twenty years old and asked the old priest about the coming battle. The sorcerer placed a round cane shield on the ground. Around it he drew a cricle and many strange symbols. Then, kneeling on the shield, the sorcerer carried on a conversation with unseen people in unintelligible words and with many wild gestures. Then he twisted his limbs and snapped the bones out of place and performed other contortions until he "looked scarcely human."

At last he calmed himself and stepped from the shield. Bowing to his leader, he revealed the number of the enemy and the place where they were waiting to fight.

All over the southeast, priests accompanied war parties and performed rituals and made warriors observe various taboos in order to assure victory. However, very little has been recorded about the Timucuan priest of battle. Doubtless a cacique who had a hundred-and-twenty-year-old sorcerer on his side was unusually lucky.

The emphasis on the torture of prisoners was the most distinctive feature of the warfare pattern of all tribes of the eastern part of North America, as compared to those of other sections. And it may be that this sadistic practice spread westward to the tribes of the Plains and the Prairies.

It has been suggested that there might have been little warfare among the aboriginal tribes before 1492 and that the American Indians learned their warring tactics from the early cruel European visitors. Anthropologists, however, seem to agree that warfare systems could and did arise independently in the Old World and in the New. Yet, the greed, cupidity, deceit, and utter disregard for Indian life on the part of most European conquerors surpassed anything of the kind that the Indian cultures had been able to produce on their own in their thousands of years of virtual independence from the Old World.

Few Stone Age peoples of the world have fought so valiantly against European intruders as did the Indians of the eastern regions of North America. Man for man, and weapon for weapon, they were more than a match for the best fighters sent against them time and time again, and only the superiority of numbers and armament brought victory to the Europeans.

Among the eastern tribes the Timucuans were one of the best and fiercest of warriors.

# CHAPTER TWELVE

# Shining Conquistadors

Some weeks later Moçoço brought the war party home. They were weary, slashed, and bruised, but shouting long before reaching the village to tell of their triumph. Enemy scalps and slaves were brought back, as well as endless tales of danger overcome by boldness and valor.

The wounded were attended to at once. Then there was a day-long ceremony of lamentation and mourning for the Timucuans who had been killed, followed by rites for their burial. These solemn rituals ended with the coming of night when drums and rattles were brought out and dancing commenced around a huge fire in the square.

Everyone in the village took part. There were victory dances by the warriors, and dances for the old, for women, and those for the pure enjoyment of the rhythm. Juan did his share of dancing, and whether participating or watching, found it all most exhilarating.

So, in dancing and feasting the night passed. The following day there was the exhibition of the war trophies and the cursing of the Calusans by the war priest. The priest's curses were terrible to hear and aroused the village to a pitch of seething hatred for their enemy.

Pooy had returned with several wounds, but none was serious, though Yua tended to them as if he were in great danger of dying. Mostly, Pooy sat around Juan's dwelling stuffing himself on choice delicacies prepared by Yua. In between these eating bouts he told again and again of his exploits and of the praise Mococo had lavished on him.

Thus the days of the raid passed into tribal memory and life returned to normal in the village. Old people died and were buried with the proper ceremonies. Children arrived with priestly blessings paid for by the parents.

Over the years Pooy and Yua had two daughters, who spent as much time with Juan as they did with their parents. It was strange for a Spaniard to teach Timucuan children Timucuan customs, but Juan did and enjoyed his share of their upbringing.

Mococo was true to his word and saw that Juan was adopted into the tribe. Then the white Timucuan accompanied the cacique on raids and willingly did whatever was demanded of him. But there was always plenty of time for his own pleasures—storytelling, singing, eating. He caught eels thick as his thigh and enjoyed the rich broth made from them. He fought alligators and roasted their meat for greedy feasts. He devoured snakes, water rats, tortoises, wild grasses. He had his arms tattooed in beautiful designs. And he became more Timucuan and less Spanish. Indian words and phrases sprang readily to his tongue as he forgot more and more of his own language. He had become as much Indian as an adopted Spaniard could be.

One day Juan was boiling deer antlers to make glue when he was told the cacique wanted him. He left Yua's older daughter to watch the pot and trotted off.

Mocoço sat on a stool in the shed where council meetings were held. The temple priest was to his right, and his advisers sat at his left, as was the custom. Juan greeted them and waited before the cacique.

"When you came to me for protection," Mocoço said, teasing the parrakeet that sat on his upraised wrist, "I promised you I would tell you whenever your countrymen were near. They are at Ucita." He paused and looked up at the Spaniard and asked, "Do you wish to join them?"

Juan stood stunned, speechless. He had been here a long time. How long he did not know. Life was good, and the Timucuans were fine people. But he was still a Spaniard in his heart; he was still a Christian, though he had not said his prayers in some time.

Mutely he nodded. How could he express such divided feelings as wanting to leave as well as wishing to stay? However, it was his duty to his church and his king that he return.

"I yearn to see my homeland and my family," he stammered at last, "since part of a man's heart is always left in the place where he was born and grew up. I must leave . . . though you and your people have been closer to me than my own kin ever were. I thank you for your many kindnesses . . . but I must leave."

A deep sadness fell on Juan. How could he tell Pooy and Yua and the little girls? How could he face leaving them?

"It is only right that you return to your land," the cacique went on softly. "I have always lived here, and I would despair if I left it to live elsewhere." He tossed the parrakeet into the air and stood up. "You owe me no thanks, for you have served me as faithfully as any of my own people. Your countrymen destroyed Ucita. If they come here, remember with favor your friends so that no harm befall us."

Juan walked away dazed, not knowing whether he had taken proper leave of the cacique and his council or not. All he knew was that Pooy and other warriors were going with him to make sure he arrived safely among the Spaniards.

Yua and the girls did not hear his news gladly. They shouted and cried and beat themselves with their fists, just as Timucuan women did when lamenting a dead kinsman. Pooy had to speak sharply to them to make them cease their grieving.

"There is much coming and going in life," Pooy said simply. "It is uncertain what will happen day to day. Look at Yua's aunt—happy one morning, killed and be-headed that afternoon. Juan came to us. Now he suddenly goes away. It is like that." He paused and added thoughtfully, "It may be that his own gods want him back."

Yua sighed resignedly and said that Juan would be remembered—the cross-god he gave to save her life, the time he shot Pooy inside a deerskin believing him a deer, the many strange things he carved for the girls to play with.

Then Pooy dragged him away quickly to where his kinsmen waited. A last look at the town, a wave to Yua, and Juan Ortiz left the town of Mocoço, sad but happy, fearful yet eager. They traveled toward Ucita at a trot but were still a good distance from the village and crossing a savanna when an uproar sounded in the thicket behind them.

They turned to see a troop of horsemen spew from the trees and scatter across the savanna toward them. "Run!" shouted Pooy, and he and the others sped toward the woods or hid among the clumps of grass.

Only Juan remained on the path, entranced at the sight of his countrymen. Sunlight glimmered around their helmets like halos and sparkled in fiery points across their steel breastplates. The great beasts pranced through the grass with flying manes and lips flecked with foam.

It was beautiful—this spectacle of armed men and horses. *Caballeros!* Spanish lancers! Shining conquistadors! His very own Christian countrymen!

A lancer separated from the others and, spurring his mount, charged straight at Juan at a hard gallop. He lowered his lance and braced the butt against the saddle. The sharp metal point, tilted at Juan's naked body, loomed closer and closer.

"Run! Run!" he heard Pooy shout.

Juan could not move, but it didn't matter. He had but to cry out Spanish words to save himself from that deadly lance. He took a deep breath and opened his lips—

He had forgotten his own language! He could not recall a single word.

# CHAPTER THIRTEEN

# Adelantado of Florida

The horse pounded on, snorting and baring its huge yellow teeth. Above the long lance the rider's face squeezed together, hard and cruel, the eyes bright with bloodshed.

Juan could not move. He could not leap away. Nor could he find words to cry out to save himself. A moment more and the spear would tear into his body.

The lancer suddenly leaned forward and yelled the Spanish battle cry, "Santiago!"

The cry was like a blow. Memories, words, images crowded into Juan's mind and jolted him into action. He thrust the unstrung bow before him and placed his right arm across it in the sign of the cross and shrieked desperately in Spanish, "Holy Mary! Slay me not!"

Astounded, the horseman managed to jerk the lance upward. Even so, the point sliced across the top of Juan's shoulder, and the iron stirrup slammed into him as the horse rushed past.

Wheeling his mount, the lancer came back warily, his spear at the ready. "How is it that you speak Castilian?"

By great effort Juan managed to answer, "Christian . . . Juan . . . Ortiz." He paused and added a word that suddenly came to him, "Sevilla! Sevilla!" and he saw that the rider understood him.

"A Christian!" The rider snorted in disbelief.

Juan understood. In his breechclout and moccasins, oiled and tattooed and decorated like any Indian, who would believe that he was a Spaniard?

"A Christian," he repeated, words coming more easily, "Juan Ortiz from Narváez's ship . . . years ago."

The lancer stared. The truth of what Juan was saying crept over him. There were shouts from the other horsemen as they beat through the grass and along the edge of the woods, looking for the Indians.

"Were those savages with you friends?" asked the lancer. Juan nodded, and the soldier called to his companions not to harm the Indians. Then he reached down a hand and pulled Juan up behind him, and they rode to the spot where the others waited.

The captain in charge was Baltasar de Gallegos, and when he heard who Juan was, he smiled. "The Governor will be delirious with joy at your coming," he said, "for we need someone who speaks the heathen's tongue."

Gallegos told Juan that the Timucuans were free to return to their village or to come back to camp with them, but that they must start back at once, for the day was late and their leader was expecting them before dark.

At Juan's call Pooy slipped from the thicket and came forward, hesitant and keeping well away from

*Above:* This woodcut, made soon after the discovery of the New World, shows King Ferdinand on his throne in Spain watching Columbus about to land among naked "savages." The men are shown with long beards, which no Indian wore.    *Below:* European seamen of the time of Columbus believed that whoever sailed west across the Atlantic would be devoured by "lurking watery horrors."

*I. N. Phelps Stokes Collection, the New York Public Library, Astor, Lenox and Tilden Foundations*

*Above:* A German woodcut showing that Europeans believed New World inhabitants to be cannibals who roasted and ate parts of their slain enemies. In this print the natives are as wooden as our own cigar-store Indians and again have beards.     *Below:* To keep game from spoiling, Timucuans smoked it on a *barbacoa*, a rack depicted here by the French artist Le Moyne. Captives were sometimes roasted on a lower *barbacoa*.

*Smithsonian Institution National Anthropological Archives*

Timucuan warriors were tall and tattooed and had bows "of the same height as he who carries them." Is that a basket hat, as some believe, or simply a hairdress?

Women planted corn in holes made in the ground with pointed sticks. Men broke clods of earth with hoes of stone or shell.

21

Stories of the Middle Ages told that in the Sea of Darkness (the Atlantic) there lurked the Biblical Leviathan—the sea serpent. It had a long, scaly body and shiny eyes and was able to snatch a sailor from a ship's deck and eat him.

When the French came among the Timucuans the second time, they found them worshiping a stone column "carved with the arms of the King of France," which had been erected by the first French newcomers to Florida.

*Above:* Each spring a deerskin stuffed with herbs was offered to the sun in a ceremony to insure a bountiful crop for the new growing season.
*Below:* Timucuan hunters stalked deer by hiding inside a deerskin and creeping across open spaces to shoot them with bows and arrows.

Before going to war, the chief prayed to the sun for victory, scattering water from a vessel as he hoped his followers would scatter the blood of their enemies.

The French artist Le Moyne depicted a sorcerer (or priest or conjurer) twisting his arms out of joint "till the bones snapped" as he went into a trance to reveal to his chief the result of a coming battle.

*Above:* This portrait of De Soto before his expedition into Florida is surrounded by pictures of conscripted Indians mining precious ores and a litter-born chieftain supervising.　　*Below:* An artist's depiction of De Soto's landing at Tampa Bay in 1539. The Gentleman of Elvas, who was there, wrote that "two hundred and thirteen horses were set on shore to unburden the ship" so they could move closer to land.

*Above:* The Timucuans of Florida pushed a sharpened pole down the throat of an attacking alligator. Then it was turned over on its back and killed by piercing its soft belly with spears and arrows. *Below:* This Le Moyne print shows young Timucuans practicing with bows and arrows, fishing, and throwing balls at a target on top of a dead tree.

the horses. He looked up at Juan and scolded his friend
for being so rash as to expose himself to the soldiers.
He might have been killed. He should have hidden
himself as he had been taught. The other Timucuans
joined Pooy and added their rebukes to his.

Juan was touched at their concern for him and
smiled at their gentle but sincere censure. He told
them that his feet had refused to run and that he had
forgotten his own language, that he could think of only
Timucuan words to call out to his countrymen. This
amused the Indians greatly, and they joked that Juan
was much too Timucuan to be taken back by the Spaniards.

Pooy sent two warriors back to Mocoço to inform
him all was well and that the rest would return the following day. Then Gallegos assigned a mounted lancer
to carry each of the Timucuans to camp, but the Indians were reluctant even to get near the horses.

Juan called encouragement and told them that it
would be like riding a log in a river. That struck the
Timucuans as highly unlikely, and they told him so,
still holding back. They wanted Pooy to get on first.

At Juan's insistence Pooy agreed. Gallegos reached
down for him. The Indian gave him his hand, and the
Spaniard jerked him astride the animal. But the horse
was startled and reared. Pooy tumbled backward to
the ground and sat there in stiff astonishment, his
mouth open, his eyes rolling, and his bundle of hair
loose with arrows dangling down around his shoulders.

He was not hurt, and as he got slowly to his feet, his
kinsmen burst out laughing. Pooy grinned weakly at

them and began to rearrange his hair. Let the others take their turn, he called out.

The lancers were enjoying the natives' first encounter with horses and looked forward to more fun on the way to the camp at Ucita. But Gallegos cautioned them not to pull any tricks and anger the Indians, lest they round up their tribesmen and attack the army, which would displease their commander.

Now Juan called out to Pooy to remember that a Timucuan warrior always faced his opponent bravely and he should try to mount again, for they must be under way at once.

Gallegos had calmed his mount and sat patiently waiting. Pooy approached slowly, and Gallegos pulled him to the horse's back once again. This time Pooy sat astride the animal's rump and looked around, pleased and proud. Now the others were eager to try.

Long before they reached the camp, they could hear the shouting, laughing, and singing of the soldiers. Closer, there came the neighing and snuffling of the horses, and finally, at the edge of camp, the squeals of pigs.

Juan could not believe his ears. Pigs? Here in Florida with the soldiers? He asked the horseman.

"Our commander brought thirteen pigs to serve as a walking food supply," the lancer replied. "They can travel as fast as the army, eat what they find, and multiply. The commander says one day the pigs will save our lives." He paused and added with admiration, "Our Don Hernando de Soto! He has thought of everything!"

They passed the pigs in a makeshift pen and their guard. Juan strained to see the beasts. He had never dreamed to behold a pig again.

Among the scattered campfires the soldiers started up as the horses walked by, each with a double burden of lancer and Indian. Questions and shouts and unbelieving exclamations rang through the camp.

Ucita's houses had been torn down, even the temple. All that remained was the mound with the cacique's dwelling. Gallegos halted his men at the foot of the mound and dismounted. He gathered Juan and the Timucuans around him.

Juan followed Gallegos up the mound steps. How strange to be here again! What a difference this time! Before he had been a captive of the infidels, awaiting torture. Now . . . now, he was— Juan knew not what he was or what lay ahead for him tomorrow, but at least for the time being he was a Christian back among his countrymen.

Pitch pine torches blazed on each side of the doorway, and a guard with a sword and buckler walked before it. "Tell the Adelantado that there are people of importance here to see him," Gallegos called to the guard.

By the time the group reached the flat top, a man dressed in velvet pants and a shirt with full-slashed sleeves stood in the hut's doorway. A greyhound on a leash was at his side. At the sight of the Indians it growled and strained toward them.

"What means this, Gallegos?"

"I have found a Christian who has lived among the

infidels these many years, Adelantado," the horseman answered. "Juan Ortiz from the expedition of Narváez." He gestured at the line of Timucuans. "These are his friends." He pushed Juan gently forward. "This is the Governor of Cuba, Adelantado of Florida, Don Hernando de Soto."

Juan looked into that thin face and those shadowed eyes, and the Spanish explorer looked back. Juan had forgotten in his years among the Indians the strange fanatic look of such a leader as De Soto; forgotten the hunger and the haunting that lay behind his eyes. But it was easily recognized once again, a light that might chill the heart as well as stir it.

Surely here was a man who in an instant would recognize that Juan Ortiz was indeed a white man, a Christian. Stained and scarred and changed as he was, once, it was clear, Ortiz had been a Spaniard and a sailor.

"Welcome, Juan Ortiz," De Soto said at last with a smile. "And glory be to God who by His goodness has sent you to us. The expedition badly needs a tongue."

He turned to his chief constable. "Gallegos, see that the Indians are taken care of and return Juan Ortiz to me as soon as he is a presentable Christian."

# INTERLUDE VI

Soto was his surname, and that is the correct way to refer to him except when his name is written out in full. However, history texts have used De Soto too long. Now it is the accepted mode.

In June of 1539, when Juan Ortiz was brought to him, De Soto was a much traveled man in the New World, though this was his first visit to Florida. He had made his fortune in the New World and returned to Spain to spend a large portion of it. To replenish his coffers and stuff a few more adventures into his life, perhaps already overfilled with hazards, he was once more back in the New World.

And why not? Spaniards considered the Americas the eighth wonder of the world. All those precious jewels, all that silver, all those golden vessels! The New World was enormous in size and had not yet been explored to its limits. More treasure lay waiting—waiting somewhere. That somewhere was Florida, De Soto believed, and he was gambling everything on his belief.

De Soto had not always been so lacking in caution.

He was born in Jerez, Spain, in 1500, it is believed, "of good origin; his blood what is called noble in Spain and so derived from the four quarterings of ancestry." Noble ancestors are not always wealthy ones, and De Soto had a rough time growing up until he found a patron to give him material aid and protection. The patron was Pedro Arias de Avila, Count of Puno en Rostro, called Pedrarias by historians.

In his younger days Pedrarias was a soldier and so good in the tilting yard that he had earned the nickname of "The Jouster." After he married the bosom friend of Queen Isabella the Catholic, he became a great courtier. Perhaps it was the queen's death that brought him disfavor at court, or bad health, or old age. Or it might have been all three that made him sour-tempered and touchy.

And then Pedrarias died. On his bier in the church awaiting burial, he revived, sat up, and was his old testy, ailing self again. Now catalepsy was added to his numerous symptoms.

So it was that King Ferdinand sent Pedrarias at the age of seventy-four to the New World. Too old for the job, disliked by many who might have been a help to him, affected with uncertain health, Pedrarias went, taking with him what one historian has described as "the most brilliant company that ever left Spain."

De Soto was along, and he was a great help to his patron, for he was a daring horseman and a keen swordsman. He did well in the New World but had not accumulated a great amount of wealth until he went with Pizarro and conquered the Incas of Peru. The treasure they took from the Indians was fabulous. De Soto's share made him wealthy enough for the king to borrow money from him.

Returning to Spain, he wed the daughter of Pedrarias. But married life at the Spanish court was dull compared to crossing dizzy Andean heights on swinging bridges and wooing Inca maidens and fighting on horseback masses of Inca Indians.

Back he came to the eighth wonder of the world—the Americas. He landed in Florida with a large expedition. His soldiers had captured at once Indian men and women to act as guides and interpreters, but all had escaped. No one wanted to push into the Floridian jungles without someone with knowledge of the country.

Then Juan Ortiz arrived, and there was great rejoicing. The one surviving letter of De Soto from Florida was written from the Tampa Bay area to his Board of Magistrates in Cuba. It says: "This interpreter puts a new life into us in affording the means of our understanding these people, for without him I know not what would become of us. Glory be to God, who by His goodness has directed all, so that it appears as if He had taken this enterprise in His special keeping, that it may be for His service, as I have supplicated, and do dedicate it to Him."

A compatriot of De Soto's has stated simply the reasons Spaniards came to the New World: "We came here to serve God and to get rich." So it was with De Soto.

# CHAPTER FOURTEEN

# The New World Interpreter

Juan stood in the firelight before his Timucuan friends, turning slowly around so they could admire the suit of velvet clothes De Soto had sent him. Pooy was not impressed, saying Yua could dress deerskins and make them that soft.

"They would never do to hunt in," Pooy added.

Juan agreed they would not. He was not even sure they were good for sitting in either. His arms and legs felt as if they were being cut in two with every little movement. There was a great deal to say for the loose, comfortable breechclout he was used to wearing.

He would have to learn to wear clothes and shoes and give up his savage ways. Staring at the shoes of stiff Spanish leather beside him, he sighed. He had been unable to squeeze his tough calloused feet into those.

Pooy was concerned about Juan's hair. It had been perfumed. The smell offended Pooy. And it had been cut much too short. "Where will you carry your arrows now?" he asked.

Juan did not answer. It seemed likely that he would
be carrying a Spanish crossbow or harquebus or a
sword of Toledo steel instead of the bow and arrow he
was now accustomed to. It seemed likely, too, that he
would have to give up a good many pleasant ways he
had learned from the Indians.

A short while ago Juan and the Timucuans had almost been killed by the Spanish lancers. Now he was
bathed and perfumed and had made his confession to
a priest. His friends were entertaining the soldiers with
Timucuan songs, and the soldiers were offering the
warriors trinkets and food in gratitude for their kindness to a Spaniard. Juan's life had been turned heels
over head.

Tomorrow the Timucuans would return to Mocoço.
And what lay ahead for Juan Ortiz? There were ships
in the bay unloading supplies, getting ready to sail
back to Cuba. Who knew but that he might be on one
of the brigantines, headed for Cuba on the first leg of
his journey back to Spain?

"Come along," Gallegos called out. "The Adelantado
is waiting with his officers to see you."

Juan glanced at his shoes and hose and shrugged. He
would have to appear before De Soto without them.
But he must get used to shoes again before he returned
to Sevilla. How his friends and family would laugh at
him coming back barefooted as a savage!

Once again he climbed the mound to Ucita's dwelling. This time he entered and was offered a chair, a
tray of sweetmeats, and a glass of wine. The comfit was
too sweet; the wine made his head swim. He listened

to the babble of voices around him. A word or phrase jogged his memory now and then. Spanish was beginning again to have its old homey flavor. Only occasionally did some word baffle him, some word he had known since babyhood but which for some reason escaped him.

Juan had never before heard of Hernando de Soto, but he could see that this was a great Spaniard, a leader like Narváez. De Soto seemed to live in a grander style. Wine and good food, furs and velvets, crystal and silver vessels—surely such a style of living would be much too splendid for Florida's mires and biting flies.

One of the company introduced himself as Rodrigo Ranjel, secretary to De Soto. He placed a folding stool beside Juan and sat down. "The Adelantado had to confer with one of the ship's captains," he said, "but he will be here shortly. I believe I heard that you came to Florida with Narváez." Then seeing that Juan looked bewildered, he repeated his words more slowly.

Juan nodded that he had been with Narváez. Ranjel continued, "That was in 1528—so you spent eleven years with the naked infidels?"

Eleven years. Eleven! More years than he had fingers. It sounded such a long time when it was said aloud. Yet, except for his time in Ucita, it did not seem long.

Speaking slowly, Ortiz said, "I was burned here in Ucita . . . on a *barbacoa* . . . like a haunch of beef."

The others had stopped their conversation and were listening to him, Juan saw. He smiled at them. "The Timucuans like their Christians well done," he went on, "and my juices were sizzling and my skin crackling when I was rescued."

He went on to tell how he was lifted from the *barba-coa* by Acuera, the beautiful daughter of the cacique who had lived in this dwelling, and how she tended to his burns so that when the skin healed, it did not draw his muscles together and make him a cripple, as might have happened without her expert care. Every day she came to doctor him and to teach him the Timucuan language. It had been a joyful time for him in spite of his hurts.

Although his telling was halting and slow, how their dark Spanish eyes softened and glowed at Juan's romantic rescue and at the great friendship that developed between the two young people of different races.

"Gallegos says your scars are terrible to behold," exclaimed one of the captains.

Juan nodded his head. "You wish to see for yourself?" he asked simply. He stood and opened his shirt and lowered his trousers.

Ranjel cried out in pity. "A solid mass of scars," he muttered. The others shook their heads in horror.

Twisting around, Juan looked at his shiny scars and ran a finger over them, a little amazed at them himself. Pulling his clothes back on, he sat again and asked about Narváez. Ranjel replied that he was dead, that only four of his expedition came out of the Florida wilderness alive.

"One of them was the factor of the expedition, Cabeza de Vaca," the secretary continued. He pointed to two officers. "Captains Gallegos and Espindola are De Vaca's kinsmen, and they were advised by him to come to Florida with the Adelantado."

"And De Vaca will rue the day he did not come with us, too," said a voice from the doorway. It was De Soto. Ranjel got up and gave his seat to the Adelantado. A page brought him a goblet of wine. He tossed it down and, turning, asked, "What do you know of golden cities, Juan Ortiz? Have the infidels mentioned them?"

Every man in the room leaned toward Juan, their greedy eyes upon him, straining to hear any mention of that magic word.

Juan glanced around at the hard faces filled with craving and shook his head and said, "No gold." A sigh traveled around the room, and the officers went back to their conversations.

Juan explained that he had not been far beyond the town of Mocoço, that the Timucuans had never mentioned great cities of gold.

De Soto snorted in disbelief. "Treasure is in Florida and we will find it," he said firmly. He tapped Juan's knee. "You . . . I want *you* to be my interpreter. You have been preserved for this purpose. The Hand of God has sheltered you."

Juan blinked, taking in the words slowly.

"I will give you a horse and clothes," the Adelantado went on. "And a share in the treasure."

Not go back to Spain? After all these years of hope and disappointment, not go back to his homeland? He lowered his eyes and caught sight of his bare feet. Not, after all, learn to wear stiff boots again?

Yet, in Sevilla, who would know him now? Who there would remember him? Perhaps his parents were dead, his friends gone away, his kinsmen unremembering. None of the many aunts and uncles and their children could he remember well. Certainly he loved none of them as he loved Yua and Pooy and their little girls.

In Sevilla who would know or care that Juan Ortiz had learned to shoot his bow and arrow so well? Or that he could fashion his own arrows and make bone heads for them? Or that he could run as fast as Pooy and just as long?

He lifted his gaze to the unblinking eyes of the man before him. Juan was certain suddenly that De Soto would not let him return to Spain anyway. The leader was determined to take with him this man who could speak Indian languages.

Juan shrugged. Why not? The New World was a vast place, and beautiful. Anywhere he turned he saw something wonderful and strange and new. He would like to see more of it. And when the exploring was done, he could return to Spain—or he might chose to go back once again to Mococo's village and its loving and happy people and the ways of living that he knew and understood.

The others could read the message in his face, that he agreed to come. Ranjel smiled and laid a hand on his shoulder, as if in welcome.

De Soto questioned him further about the country

and what to expect. Juan answered as best he could. Then the Adelantado dismissed him, saying he must dictate a letter to his secretary. The letter would go to those left in charge at Cuba and tell them all was well with the expedition.

Gallegos was waiting outside the cacique's house. "I'll take you to your camp," he said, gesturing toward the flickering campfires.

Juan looked over the fires toward the rim of darkness that marked the jungle. He had an idea that Pooy and the others were sleeping there, not close to one of the white men's fires. "Thank you," he answered Gallegos, "I can find my own way." And before the captain could say anything else, he slipped away into the shadows.

# CHAPTER FIFTEEN

# Mocoço's Visit

Now that there was an interpreter to deal with the Indians, the soldiers were eager to begin their search for treasure. The Adelantado was even more impatient to leave, but first plans had to be made and the march organized.

A brigantine was dispatched northward along the Florida coast to find a good harbor where supply ships could rendezvous with the army. Other vessels returned to Cuba with instructions about food that would be needed in the future and with letters from the soldiers to their wives and friends.

De Soto sent Captain Gallegos northward with a body of cavalry and foot soldiers, with orders to seize food and villages for the army's use. Officers kept the men busy checking their weapons and equipment, for everyone had to be ready to march on quick notice.

The Timucuans left the camp carrying a great load of presents. They had seen everything and wanted to go home and tell of their adventures and describe the peculiar customs of these newcomers. Pooy took back a message from De Soto, asking Mocoço to visit the camp at Ucita. The Adelantado wanted to thank him for his kind treatment of Juan Ortiz. But more than that, he wanted to impress the cacique with the strength of his army and its weapons. The Spaniards must pass through Mocoço's territory on their way north. De Soto would make sure that the cacique realized that it was to his advantage to remain on good terms with the invaders.

Juan watched all the preparations with as much interest as any of the savages. He was amazed at the amount of stores that were to travel with this large expedition. There were all manner of tools to repair weapons and armor, blacksmith anvils and bellows, tailors' kits, and extra pieces of equipment, as well as tents, chains, ropes, and chests of clothes. So well prepared was the expedition, Hernando de Soto must surely find the golden cities of Florida, no matter how far he had to seek.

At first Juan wore a loose robe. Then he tried a linen shirt, and though it scratched, he soon was used to it. Breeches took longer, for they hindered his movements as if his legs were wrapped in coils of rope. But boots and shoes he refused to wear. They not only blistered his feet but also were awkward to walk in. He much preferred heelless moccasins.

One morning a group of Timucuans arrived. They had come to build an arbor for Mocoço to sit under when he talked to the Adelantado. The cacique's carved wooden stool was with them. Juan told De Soto this was the custom of a cacique visiting another

leader. Since there was no knowing how many followers Mocoço might bring, an open-sided arbor would be
better than the mound dwelling for a meeting and also
cooler.

De Soto told Juan to help the Indians choose a place
for the structure and promised that he and his officers
would be ready to give the cacique a royal welcome.

The Indians found a site to their liking near the
beach and away from the soldiers' quarters. They set to
work with their stone tools to cut saplings, which were
placed upright in the ground on the sides. Then canes
were tied with vines from one upright to another to
form a framework at the top. Canes were laid for the
roof. This shade arbor was quickly erected and Mocoço's stool placed at one end. A page brought the Adelantado's chair and set it at the opposite end.

Juan had just put on his velvet suit when he heard
the approaching musicians. He hastened to the arbor
to find De Soto and several of his officers. Harquebusiers were lined up along the path, and soldiers were
running up to watch the Indian procession.

The musicians came first playing cane flageolets and
making a great deal of noise but little music. After
them were armed warriors. Next was Mocoço in a
white feather mantle with the skin of a blackbird on
his head. On his right was the temple priest, while his
chief councilor was on his other side. Mocoço's wives
followed, and behind them more warriors.

As the cacique neared the arbor, the harquebusiers
fired their guns. The smoke and noise brought a startled pause in the music, and the temple priest ap-

peared uneasy, but Mocoço was delighted with the salute. He entered the arbor and solemnly stood before his stool, his followers ranged around him.

Juan stepped between the two leaders and in Timucuan introduced them. Mocoço came forward and took the Adelantado by the wrists and then the elbows, squeezing them affectionately. Placing his right hand over De Soto's heart, he rubbed gently and spoke greetings.

The cacique greeted Juan in the same courteous fashion and asked him to introduce each of the officers and tell him their importance. Juan did, and then the two leaders took their seats. De Soto welcomed the cacique and spoke of all Spaniards' friendship for him and thanked him for his many kindnesses to Ortiz.

Mocoço made light of his benevolence, saying that great men should always be kind to those less fortunate, especially strangers.

Talking and feasting went on all that day and the following till Juan was groggy from shifting back and forth between Timucuan and Spanish. Warfare against the Calusans had not been as grueling and wearisome. Words in Spanish still gave him trouble, and sometimes even when he understood the Spaniards, how explain unfamiliar things to the Indians?

At last Mocoço and his retinue left with their presents, and life was easier for Juan. He spent much time with the soldiers, especially those from Sevilla, asking for any news of his kin and the last-heard gossip of marketplaces.

One day a message arrived from Captain Gallegos,

and news quickly spread through the camp that he had heard of a province where it was summer the year round and there was so much gold that the Indians went to war wearing golden hats like casques. There was great excitement on hearing this and much scurrying about. De Soto immediately issued orders: they would march the following morning.

So it came about that five weeks after he joined the expedition, Juan saddled his horse, tied his extra clothes and his bow and arrows behind the saddle, and rode from Ucita at the side of De Soto, heading northward through the hot July sun.

Behind him he left the ocean, that high road to Cuba and thence back to Spain. He left the village of Mocoço and all the friends he had made, the house he had built for himself, the life he had come to love.

And ahead of him—what lay ahead?

# INTERLUDE VII

Never had an expedition set out to explore and conquer in the New World with such high hopes, such assurance, and such enthusiasm as that of Hernando de Soto. There was an air of success about the undertaking right from its very beginning.

And why not? De Soto had already been very successful once. He had returned to Spain with both prestige and wealth from his exploits in Peru. He had energy, experience, confidence, charm, and a burning desire for still more success.

What better leader can an expedition have than a rich, famous one who can skillfully handle a lance and a sword? One who stakes his possessions and his life on a venture into the wilds of Florida to gain greater fame and wealth? With such a leader there can hardly be any doubt about the success of his venture. So it seemed in the late 1530's in Spain.

If there were any doubts, these were dispelled by Cabeza de Vaca, one of the few survivors of Narváez's ill-fated Florida expedition. He never did declare that he had heard of or found any treasure trove while crossing Florida. All he said was that he had sworn not to divulge certain knowledge. If hard pressed with questions, De Vaca excused himself from answering by murmuring that certain facts were "reserved for the ear of the Emperor."

Thus it was by hints and silences, by nods and winks, that De Vaca intimated that Florida was the most likely place to go if a young man wanted to make his fortune. He even encouraged two of his kinsmen to go with De Soto. He himself would not go, for he was seeking an independent command in another New World province.

If De Soto's former good fortune did not set minds whirling with gold fever, then De Vaca's air of mystery about Florida did. And men clamored to enlist for the Florida conquest when the recruiting books were opened in Spain on January 26, 1538. They continued to join throughout February, and by the middle of March De Soto had six hundred and fifty members for his expedition; more than enough, for the Spanish king had granted him the governorship of Florida if he raised no more than five hundred men in Spain.

Such a quick, easy enlistment as De Soto's was rare. Commanders quite often had a great deal of trouble signing up a full complement. Narváez was plagued by a shortage of recruits and managed to find only three hundred willing to explore Florida with him.

There is disagreement among historians and chroniclers about the final actual number of De Soto's expedition landing in Florida. Some lists seem not to include servants and slaves whose talents were considered necessary to gentlemen abroad as well as at home. The few Spanish women who accompanied their husbands were not noted on most tallies. Other lists did not number the sailors. Perhaps these seamen heard too many tales of gold and of the wonders of Florida while sailing from their supply base at Cuba to the landing site at Tampa Bay and asked De Soto to be "land stowaways" with his expedition. Perhaps De Soto remembered how Narváez had to build boats to try to save his expedition. Whatever the reason for their inclusion, several sailors were members of De Soto's army.

All in all, a good round figure of seven hundred members can be assumed to have composed the expedition at Tampa Bay after the ships returned to Cuba. Of course, later, as Indian men and woman were added on the march, to carry baggage and to cook, the total number reached probably nine hundred to a thousand. It is no wonder this huge army frightened some Indians into hiding or that those who did not hide were appalled at the task of feeding these visitors.

At least half of the group's enlistment in Spain came from De Soto's own province of Estremadura, and most of the rest from the other districts of Spain. However, there were nineteen Portuguese along, one of whom is known only as the Knight of Elvas. He wrote the best of the four narratives we know today about the expedition.

Somehow or other, one Englishman managed to serve with De Soto's army. It is reported that he was unwilling to give up his longbow for a Spanish weapon and was not required to do so. Here, then, was one soldier with a weapon equal to the Indian bow in range and power, for the Spanish harquebus and crossbow were certainly not.

Never had there been such a well-organized Spanish expedition in the New World as that of Hernando de Soto. Even from the partial list of occupations, it can be seen that the Adelantado of Florida went prepared for almost any eventuality that might arise in the wilds far from his supply ships. There were a number of tailors, a shoemaker, a sword cutler, a calker, a carpenter, a stocking maker, and a farrier. There were two Genoese engineers and several notaries. To Christianize the Indians and perform religious services, twelve priests accompanied the army. Eight of these were clerics and four friars.

Of course the greatest number were soldiers. The elite of the fighting men were the horsemen, the *caballeros*. An ancient Spanish law decreed that *caballeros* should ride on horseback "as honor and tradition demanded." Originally, *caballero* meant only "a rider on a horse," but by the time of De Soto's expedition, it had come to mean "gentleman." Not only did possession of a horse elevate a Spaniard, but it also entitled him to a horseman's share of conquered treasure.

The horse was the single most valuable possession of a soldier, and bought in the New World, it might cost as much as six thousand dollars, though generally it was difficult to buy one at any price. Such a price was sixty times that of a good sword.

The horseman's main weapon was the lance, a

twelve-foot spear with a leaf-shaped steel head. He also carried a double-edged sword to use when the enemy pressed close and his long lance was inadequate.

There were many kinds of foot soldiers with De Soto. Of these the least useful were the pikemen whose sixteen-foot spears furnished little service against the Indians. Troops of pikeman formed the bulk of European infantry forces and so were a part of every New World army, too.

A targeteer was efficient only in hand-to-hand combat. Still, with his sword and round metal target (also called buckler or shield), this infantryman had value as a guard of supplies, of pigs, or of officers' quarters.

The halberdier used a long spear with a sharp point, below which was an axhead on one side of the shaft and opposite it a hook. The halberd was very versatile, for it could be wielded for sticking, chopping, or snaring an enemy or his weapons with the hook.

There were two types of foot soldiers with projectile arms. One was the crossbowman. His weapon, the crossbow, had been invented to shoot a missile with enough force to penetrate Old World armor. The steel bow was fitted to a wooden stock. It took some mechanical means, such as a windlass, to bend the bow so that the bow cord could be caught in firing position. It was a slow process, and though the four-headed quarrel, or arrow, once fired, killed any Indian it struck, the crossbow was much too cumbersome a weapon for wilderness warfare in southeastern America.

The only firearm the Spaniards brought with them was the harquebus, the second of the projectile weapons carried by infantry troops. It was fired by bringing a lighted slow match into contact with the priming powder, which exploded and fired the lead bullet in the gun's barrel. The harquebusier wore a long rope wick coiled around his body. The end of this had to be kept lighted and ready to fire the weapon. The smoke from this wick and the noise from the discharged gun might have frightened the southeastern Indians on their first contact with it. Mostly the savages held the weapon in contempt, a deserved attitude for such a heavy, unwieldy fighting arm.

It took about two minutes to load and fire an harquebus, during which time the Indian could probably shoot as many as twenty-five to thirty arrows and get these away with great accuracy. With the harquebus, accurate aiming was impossible. One advantage it did have, however, was that the Indians could not see its bullet in time to dodge it as the savage was able to do with the arrow fired from the crossbow.

Besides the horse and the pig, the Spaniards brought another animal with them to America—the dog. There has been discussion over whether these animals were bloodhounds or Irish greyhounds. Whatever they were, they had been trained to hate Indians, and De Soto used his dogs to run down escaped Indian slaves or to tear to pieces obstinate captives.

Juan Ponce de León was probably the most vicious of all the conquistadors in his treatment of Indians. The Spanish word *aperrear*, meaning "to cast to the dogs," made its appearance in the early 1500's when

Juan Ponce was using his dogs to subdue Indian tribes in the West Indies. He, as well as other Spanish leaders, placed his dogs on the payroll at a crossbowman's pay.

There was no set dress for De Soto's troops, and the soldiers came to Florida with a variety of armor, the kind depending upon the affluence and taste of the wearer. They might have protected their bodies with a shirt of chained mail, a gorget, or a breastplate and backpiece. Steel helmets covered their heads and necks.

In time, as their armor rusted, the soldiers, and De Soto himself, came to wear a loose garment of canvas stuffed with cotton. This was effective against Indian arrows, for it broke the force of the missiles and kept them from penetrating into the flesh. Rodrigo Ranjel, the private secretary of De Soto, in his narrative of the expedition, says that the Adelantado had him "draw out more than twenty arrows which he bore fastened in his armour, which was a loose coat quilted with coarse cotton."

This protection proved a blessing to the Spaniards, for Indian arrows could pierce thin steel armor. And when a cane arrow struck a mailed shirt, the end of the cane splintered into several pieces, each going through the metal rings of the garment into the flesh to make a most deadly wound.

Not all the members of the expedition left Spain with fine armor, however. Here is a comment from the Gentleman of Elvas on the soldiers appearing before

De Soto in Spain: "The greater number of the Castilians were in very sorry and rusty shirts of mail; all wore steel caps or helmets, but had very poor lances."

For food, besides the pigs, only wine and cassava bread are mentioned by the chroniclers. For sustenance, then, the army depended almost from the first on the country through which they traveled—or, at any rate, on the Indians who lived there.

But other supplies they brought with them. It would be many years later before explorers and colonizers of the American continent realized that the land around them could supply most of their needs—weapons, shelter, clothes, food, tools.

So the craftsmen carried with them the tools of their trade and the stuff on which to use these tools, the soldiers carried their weapons and their extra weapons, the *caballeros* brought their necessities and their luxuries. No wonder they needed so many Indians for bearers.

They must have been a strange sight bumbling through the great green woods and savannas, like a line of grotesque ants, wandering around looking for treasure, while treasure lay thick all around them—the new-found land of America.

# CHAPTER SIXTEEN

# First Adventures

Within a week of leaving Ucita the mood of the army changed. Gone now were the high spirits, the cheerfulness, the jokes. What had appeared to be little more than a pleasure jaunt across Florida turned sour with reality. The New World, which had recently seemed a golden coin to be quickly pocketed, was found to be made of base metal.

They sloshed through swamps and muddy wastes and were never dry, night or day. Eaten by mosquitoes and sucked by leeches, men and horses alike were in foul temper as they pushed northward. Only the pigs grunted along at the army's rear, contented with the forage and not minding the mud and water a bit.

July was hot and August worse. De Soto's steward died of heat prostration. Those in armor suffered terribly, but they were afraid to take off so much as their helmets for fear of the wild natives. Indians appeared without warning out of thin swampy mists and shot barrages of arrows into the army's midst and vanished before an answering volley could be given them. Harquebuses were too clumsy and slow firing to fight ambushing Indians, and crossbows were hardly better.

When the savages stayed to give battle, the Spaniards were amazed at the way they used trees as protection. They would hug a trunk to themselves, putting their arms around it to shoot their bows and arrows. How could Christians fight such unchivalrous warriors?

Juan, riding at the head of the column, was alert for figures lurking in the shadows beside the path, knew what had frightened a herd of deer that crossed their course or caused a bird to scold. He could save those close to him from being caught unaware, but those behind he could not help, for the army was strung out single file for almost a league.

At Ucita Juan had tried to warn the Spaniards that they should expect hardships, but few had heeded him. Greed had closed tight their ears and dulled their wits against truth. What would a white savage who had seen so little of Florida know of its broad expanses? Now they almost hated his cheerfulness, his patience at searching through the marshy muck for a lost trail. But the slow, slogging work of moving armored soldiers, horses, and equipment through mud, water, and thick underbrush bothered him not at all. In fact, he had never been better off in his life. He was now accustomed to long hours in the saddle—though the first days of riding had made him sore—and atop his mount he watched the landscape roll past with delight. Life among the Timucuans had trained his eyes to notice and appreciate his surroundings, and there was much to interest him.

They came on crystal springs filled with fish and turtles, all moving through the sunlit waters outlined in glittering rainbow colors. Even the ugly, scaly alligators shimmered with beautiful reds and oranges and violets in the pure water. There were fountains boiling up white sand and shell from the limestone darkness below; meadows of butterflies; the yellow flash of a panther stalking through the hammocks; and cool woods where the trees dripped with orchids.

It was useless to point these things out to his companions. This was no sightseeing expedition. Their tempers were short, jokes were few, and grumbling constant.

One day a cavalry squad returned with a few Indians for Ortiz to question. The army was glad for a chance to rest for a while in the shade. De Soto sat his horse in the August sun, stiff and patient, the plume in his casque hanging limply on his shoulder.

Juan greeted the three men in a friendly fashion. He told them not to be afraid. He asked if there was any sickness in their families, how the hunting had gone lately, and if their corn crops had thrived.

They answered politely but shifted about, ill at ease and occasionally sliding their eyes to catch a glimpse of the horses and the Spanish weapons.

"Have they told you anything yet?" asked the Adelantado at last.

Juan shook his head. De Soto never understood that

it took time and patience to get information from Indians. The talk could not be rushed. He saw the three staring at the Indian bearers chained together, and he assured them it would not happen to them. All he wanted was information, and then they were free to go. The Indians thought a bit and then squatted, for this was the position in which talk went best, they felt.

Juan dropped down with them and inquired where this path went. They replied that it led to a province called Apalache, but ended there, for there were no paths beyond. Long ago a white army had tried to get through Apalache but had failed and turned back to the nearby coast. They had sailed away in boats they made themselves.

Juan told the Adelantado what was said. "That would be Panfilo de Narváez," De Soto mused.

A few foot soldiers who had gathered to listen moaned on hearing this. "Adelantado, let us not go on," they begged the leader, "or we will end up as dead as Narváez. Let us return to Ucita while we still have food and life to get there."

Others voiced their agreement with this, but most stood silent and depressed. The Governor let them have their say, for he always listened to complaints, but when they had finished, he said simply, "For my part, I will never return till I see with my own eyes the incredible things found in Apalache."

Only a few days before, an Indian had told Juan about Apalache, saying that the province had such big fields of maize that it took days to cross them, that the warriors were much bigger than other Indians—giants who had all the gold they needed. These were the incredible things De Soto spoke of.

"I would hate to give up only a few leagues short of such a rich province," he added.

The men got to their feet without being ordered; the officers returned to their places, knowing their leader had made up his mind to go to Apalache. He always listened to their complaints, gravely and as if considering every word. But in the end it was what he wanted to do that mattered.

They moved on following the trail from village to village through the territory of the Timucuans. At each one the Adelantado demanded of its cacique food and men to serve as burden bearers. These bearers were chained together and stayed with the army until another set of bearers was found to take their places. If a cacique refused either food or men, De Soto did not hesitate to take him along on the march.

An important Timucuan cacique had traveled with the Spaniards for some time. Again and again his followers would visit De Soto and demand his release. Each time the Adelantado assured the envoys that the cacique was not a prisoner but a guest escorting the Spaniards safely through the province.

Through the heat of September the soldiers dragged along past deserted towns and maize fields burned by Indians fleeing from them. Dust hung in the air, clotted in their throats and on their sweaty bodies. About the middle of the month they reached fields in which the maize stood ungathered. In the distance was a town. Beyond it a lake gleamed.

This was a cheering sight. Now the soldiers could expect a full stomach for a change. There might even be fish in the lake. Certainly they could wash the dust of Florida from their clothes and bodies.

Juan was leading his horse as he walked beside one of the Timucuan bearers. The Indian had once been a captive of the Calusans but escaped just as he was about to be tortured. He and Juan had much to talk about and had become good friends.

"What is the Timucuan town ahead of us?" asked Juan.

"Napetaca," the bearer replied. Then lowering his voice, he added, "Beware, friend, for there is an ambush planned for you and your companions beside the lake."

Juan thanked him and mounted. Riding to the head of the column, he told the Adelantado of the attack. De Soto nodded and pushed on. At the edge of the deserted town a messenger waited. He begged De Soto to bring the captured cacique to the banks of the lake to talk to a few of his followers about his release. No one would be armed. The Spanish army was to remain on this side of the town, for there were no Indian warriors near and De Soto would be safe.

The Adelantado agreed to the meeting, and the messenger left. He halted the army with orders to wait in place. Dismounting, he called his officers to him and told of the ambush. He unstrapped his sword and handed it and his lance to his page. Then he added the dirk from his waist.

The captains begged him not to go. It was too risky.

The soldiers would not be able to reach him in time to protect him. But the Adelantado would not listen.

"I will take the trumpeter with me," he told them. "At the first sign of the attack, he will blow a call. You come then and come quickly. I will lay hold of the cacique to shield me from arrows."

Then he told where he wanted the lancers placed and the many squadrons of foot soldiers. Most of the slow-moving crossbowmen and those with harquebuses were to stay and guard the baggage and the pigs.

He dusted off his armor with a silk handkerchief and then tried to make the plume on his helmet stand erect as it once had. It was no use. The feather drooped sadly. He laughed and, turning to his captains, said, "I trust that you will be more alert than this poor plume."

But few of them smiled in response to his joke. Besides the trumpeter, De Soto chose Juan and four others to accompany him. With the cacique at his side, De Soto stepped off through the town with cocksure strides.

Juan threw his mount's reins to De Soto's page. Captain Gallegos grabbed his arm. "Ortiz," he said urgently, "don't let him wait too long to sound the trumpet. You know how foolhardy he is."

"Have no fear, Captain," Juan answered. "I am eager to get back safely myself."

But as he ran after the Adelantado, he was not without fear. He knew the Timucuans. Was this the time they were going to be avenged on the Spaniards and their reckless leader?

# CHAPTER SEVENTEEN

⑤⑨ ⑤⑨ ⑤⑨

# Loose Spanish Teeth

On the banks of the lake waited ten unarmed Indians. Trees crowded close behind them, almost to the water. It took no great wisdom to know that the rest of the Timucuans were hidden there in the woods, but De Soto strode on as if unaware of that possibility.

"Adelantado"—Juan spoke softly—"it would be best if we stopped here and let them come to us. Warriors are in the woods."

De Soto paused. "Very well," he agreed, and they halted. Juan called out, "Greetings, Timucuans, rulers of this land. We come to listen solemnly to your words."

The Indians motioned for them to come closer. The cacique stepped forward, but De Soto seized him by the arm.

"We have brought our guest, your beloved leader," Juan went on quickly. "Do you not want to come and pay your respects to him?"

The Indians hesitated. They whispered among themselves and then came slowly forward and saluted their cacique. One of them began to talk about joining the

Spaniards in warfare against the Apalaches. But the cacique was needed to organize the attack. As he spoke, the other natives began to encircle the Spaniards.

Juan, who could interpret all this without really listening, glanced toward the woods. Wasn't that a painted face peering out? Wasn't that a movement in that bush? He warned De Soto, who struggled to keep his grip on the cacique, for two of the Indians were trying to pull him away.

A war cry sounded from the woods, and the Indians burst out, brandishing war clubs, screaming, pouring across the sandy lake shore.

"Sound the trumpet!" snapped De Soto.

But no call came. Ortiz looked around and saw a Timucuan holding the bell-shaped end of the instrument, trying to take it from the trumpeter. Juan pushed through the scuffling, swaying bodies and kicked the Timucuan, who released the trumpet, turning in anger. Juan knocked him to the ground and kicked him again, shouting for the trumpeter to blow quickly or they were all lost.

Gallegos had feared for his leader and had already ordered the cavalry out of the cover of the village. The horses thundered down the slope, and the cry rang out, "Santiago! Santiago!"

The Indians around De Soto and his men broke and ran. At last the trumpet sounded a tattered, uneven call, and the infantry charged from their scattered hiding places. De Soto dragged the cacique clear of the melee. A page had brought up a horse for him, and De Soto pushed the Indian at Ortiz and mounted swiftly.

He galloped off to join the battle, screaming as wildly as his lancers.

Juan held the cacique, who was now making no effort to escape. It had been risky for the Spaniards, and, as always, De Soto had gambled on his courage and good luck to overcome the risks.

An old Castilian proverb said, "It is foolish to fear what cannot be avoided." As De Soto's interpreter, Juan could not avoid taking chances when it was the Adelantado's wish. But the Spanish leader seemed to take too many chances, to be reckless with his own, as well as other lives. For a city of gold? What good would it do a dead man?

Juan pushed the cacique ahead of him through the twilight toward the huts, for his part in the fight was over.

A great number of Timucuans were killed; the rest escaped into the lake, hoping to slip away later in the dark. But the Adelantado had fires built at intervals around the lake. Between these he placed his horsemen.

All night long the Indians swam in the deep water at the center of the lake. A few tried to escape by floating to the bank underneath lily pads, but the lancers killed them. Ortiz walked from fire to fire calling out over the water for the Timucuans to surrender and they would not be harmed. They held out till daylight; then all waded out but one young warrior who had to be dragged out by force.

The captives were herded to the town and thrown into the huts, their arms tied, and soldiers set to guard them. The Spaniards stayed at the lake washing their wounds and hoping for a long day's rest.

De Soto came out of his tent set up in the town square. Ortiz was with him. They were to inspect the prisoners, some of whom would be given to officers as servants. Others would be chained together in iron collars to carry the army's food. The caciques from the different villages and other leaders would be used as hostages to insure safe travel through the country.

As they walked along the streets in the bright morning light, a pig suddenly shot from between two dwellings, squealing with all its might. Behind the animal came a man, yelling curses and calling on the pig to stop.

Juan laughed. But the Adelantado was not amused. "Soldier," he shouted, "I will have you quartered if that pig gets away."

He stood watching the chase with his hands on his hips. "Someday we will need every pig we have to save us from starving," he said. "A dozen may go hungry for lack of that pig."

They went on through the deserted streets and stopped at a house where two men with swords and bucklers guarded the doorway. De Soto entered and looked around at the savages, some sitting, others leaning against the walls. One of those standing was a tall, handsome warrior with many tattoos on his face and body. Juan pointed him out. "That one—he is a cacique."

De Soto nodded. "Cut his bonds and we'll interview him outside."

Ortiz slipped his dagger from its sheath and slashed the ropes. With a wild scream the Indian pushed Juan aside and leaped at the Adelantado and struck him heavily in the face with his fist. The other captives joined the attack, swinging their bound arms and butting and biting. The two guards dashed inside and hacked at the prisoners with their swords, but the Indians swarmed over them and pressed them to the floor.

Blood was streaming from De Soto's nose and mouth. He battered at his assailant with his fists and kicked him with the hard toe of his boot and was getting the best of the fight when Camp Master Moscoso rushed inside and drove his sword into the Timucuan.

De Soto pushed through the doorway, and Ortiz scrambled after him. Blood bubbled from the Adelantado's mouth. He leaned over and spat. Then he felt his teeth, and Juan saw that the front ones were very loose in their sockets.

Shouting and confusion filled the streets. Throughout the town the captives were streaming from the huts, some with swords and lances in their hands. It was a revolt.

"To arms! To arms!" cried a soldier as he ran past Ortiz.

Soldiers came running from all directions, half armed and undressed, and were amazed to find that the natives had control of the town. The Indian burdeners had joined the new captives, and they fought with chains, bridles, burning brands, pikes—anything they could find for weapons.

De Soto and Ortiz started for the square, but the

maddened savages pressed around them. A squad of halberdiers came to their aid, and then Camp Master Moscoso arrived with pikemen and crossbowmen and took charge of the revolt.

The Indians were at last subdued, one by one recaptured and placed in chains. The greyhounds were turned loose to rip to pieces the worst offenders. Others were shot to death by the crossbowmen in the square. Some of these soldiers were repulsed at such slaughter. They did not mind killing in a battle, armed man against armed man, but this was not for true soldiers. Others cared little for the infidels and carried out the execution orders without a qualm.

De Soto stood near his tent with the soldiers, watching the Indians killed. Some of his followers stared at his bloody nose and puffy lips in awe, as if they had not known one so great could bleed and bruise like common fighters.

Gallegos sent the Adelantado's chamberlain for the priest and his medicine chest to doctor the leader's hurts. De Soto had not lost any teeth from the blow, but it would be many days before he would be able to chew any food.

De Soto turned to his constable. "Gallegos, you know how the lords of the King's Council are always imploring us to treat the infidels with gentleness," he snapped. "I would to God they had been here to see what we go through to serve His Majesty. Gentle the savages and they bite the hand that pets them." He touched his mouth tenderly, adding, "Or loosen all one's teeth."

Some of the soldiers who heard this muttered among themselves. Since there was no gold to be found, it was useless to stay here and keep on fighting. It would be best for all if they left this land now and let the devil-worshiping savages have it. They were weary of Florida and its hardships.

But now there would be no leaving, no rest for them. The Adelantado was angry, and he would keep them killing Indians till the land was colored with their dying blood and he was appeased for his hurts.

Only Juan Ortiz was not worried about tomorrow. Stay or go—it was all the same to him.

🔲🔲 🔲🔲 🔲🔲

# CHAPTER EIGHTEEN

# Winter Quarters in Apalache

The Adelantado was greatly pleased with the province of Apalache and took over its capital in late October for winter quarters. The soldiers were glad. There was an abundance of maize, beans, pumpkins, and dried fruits in the Indian storehouses. Deer and small game were easily killed among the glades and hardwood hammocks, and since they were not too many leagues from the sea, fish and crab were available for fasting days.

It would have been an idyllic winter except for the Apalache Indians. They were not the giants other Indians reported them to be, but they were extremely fierce and unrelenting in their harassment of the Spaniards. If one soldier went from the town to cut firewood or to fish in the nearby river, a dozen men had to go along to guard him from attack. Day and night the Apalaches pestered the Spaniards, killing a soldier here, a horse there, making quick sorties of destruction against the town and its guards and escaping unharmed.

In spite of the danger Juan managed to hunt deer with his bow far from the town. He had lost some of his skill, but he still enjoyed the chase and seldom came back to camp empty-handed. He smoked the deer hides and made himself several pairs of moccasins. He offered to make them for soldiers who were wearing delapidated boots. But his offer was refused. Who would wear an infidel's shoes?

There were several priests with the expedition, and they welcomed being in these more permanent quarters. An altar was erected in one of the huts and mass said daily. The fathers had a mold in which to make the holy wafers for Communion services and cases of sacramental wine to offer in a silver chalice.

The soldiers and the craftsmen were a varied group, and many of them had traveled to the far-off corners of the Spanish colonies of the New World. They had seen much and were not hesitant to share their experiences with their companions. Cold nights were spent huddled close to fires as these travelers told of strange things—holes in the earth so deep that the fires of hell could be seen at their bottoms; in the Andes Mountains violent winds that took away a man's hands and feet; drinking cups cut from one large emerald; apples that turned into worms. The tales were endless, for when one finished, another took his place.

There was also quieter talk of the king and his court and of Spain's rival for colonies and treasure—Portugal. Sometimes one of the priests told stories of the saints and their hardships in the long ago times when Christianity was only one of many religions in the Roman

Empire. Juan was more of a listener than a talker, but he was often urged to tell what he knew of the Floridians and sometimes did.

Though the soldiers listened with interest and sometimes with wonder, few of them had much patience with Juan's liking for the Indians and their way of living. The Spaniards were convinced that the savages were little more than the beasts of the fields, eating raw food and living in filth.

Ortiz was always astonished. Even while they were living in this pleasant village, made and occupied by the Indians, they still thought this. It was useless to argue, and he did not try.

De Soto sent to Ucita for the rest of the soldiers. Part of them came to Apalache by land, the rest on a brigantine. After its arrival, the ship was sent westward along the coast to find a good harbor and land suitable for settlement. This pleased many, for they had come to believe that Florida was empty of treasure, of gold and jewels. It must yield some other form of wealth, and they were now thinking of leaving the expedition to farm with their Indian slaves.

The brigantine returned, reporting that a fine port with deep water lay to the west not too far distant in a land the Indians called Achuse. Now the soldiers spent their leisure time discussing their future opportunities, not recalling the past. When the army marched to the harbor, would they take ship and return to the Spanish settlement in Cuba? Or Spain? Or would they stay and help found the first Spanish colony in Florida?

Juan made no speculations. He lived day to day. It

was the best way in the New World. Anyway, De Soto had not made known his plans for the army yet. With such a one, who knew what tomorrow might bring?

It was a hot, sunny day in February, and soldiers lazied about their quarters, reluctant to stir far from shade. Except for a few Indian women pounding corn in mortars before the huts, Juan had the town streets to himself. He had left his horse at the blacksmith's for a new shoe and then set out to hunt.

But someone called his name as he walked. He turned to find De Soto's page running toward him. "The Adelantado wants you at once," he said, panting. "And Gallegos as well. Have you seen him?"

"At the smith's," Juan replied. "What is happening? What is the great rush?"

"Gold!" The page grinned. "Is there ever anything else of importance happening?" He ran on.

The Adelantado was always impatient, he always wanted people to come running. But Juan did not hurry. It was hot. If there was gold, it could wait.

Crossing the square, he saw Captain Gallegos entering the cacique's house at the far end. He quickened his steps, and at the doorway the guard waved him inside.

"Excellency," said Juan hesitantly, unable to see after the brightness outside.

"Ortiz!" cried De Soto. "You must find out the truth for us. It is important. This young savage belongs to my treasurer, and we believe he is telling us of . . ."

The treasurer of the expedition interrupted. "Adelantado," Juan Gaytan said, "why not let the interpreter find out for himself and see if he is of one mind with us?"

De Soto nodded in agreement and then pointed. "Question the Indian closely."

A young Indian stood beside a table, shifting about uneasily. He wore a breechclout and a torn linen shirt. Juan moved over and began to talk to him in soft tones. The boy babbled in reply, jerking his arms wildly around. After a while he quieted, but Juan still had trouble understanding since the Indian knew only a few Timucuan words.

The best that Juan could get from the youth was that he lived toward the rising sun in a province ruled by a woman. He had been captured and sold to the Timucuans, from whom he was taken by the Spaniards. Now he wanted to return to his home. He would guide the army there. In the woman's province was much metal—he snatched up a ring from the table and shook it in Juan's face—much metal like this.

The boy became much too excited then to talk, but he went through many gestures and movements, trying to explain something to Juan.

"See!" exclaimed De Soto, an edge of excitement in his voice. "He is plainly showing us how the gold is dug up and how big lumps of it are taken and pounded with clubs. The gold is so pure, it does not have to be melted and refined. The impurities are beaten out, leaving the metal in thin sheets. I saw Inca Indians doing the very same thing in Peru."

It might be that was what the Indian was trying to show them. And Indians could indeed beat gold into sheets, or roots into meal, or an enemy into subjection.

Ortiz turned to De Soto. "The boy is not Timucuan, so I do not understand all he says," he declared. "I am only certain that his home is to the east in a country ruled by a woman and that he wants to guide the army there." He paused, doubtful whether to mention gold or not. "It . . . it may be gold he is telling us about, I cannot say."

"Or it may be copper, or something else," grunted Gallegos.

De Soto whirled around, his eyes hard. "What think you, Captain, if the army marches east to the woman's province to see about this gold?"

"I think the soldiers will be disappointed not to go westward to the harbor at Achuse," Gallegos replied pointedly.

"And you yourself, Captain Gallegos—what do you think?"

"I do not think. I go with you as always, Adelantado," came the quiet reply.

De Soto relaxed. "Good," he said. "Begin preparations at once. When all is ready, we go east—for *gold*, tell the men."

Gallegos and Ortiz left. As they walked across the square, the captain said angrily, "You might have told De Soto the boy is lying." He stopped and snatched at Juan's shoulder. "He was lying, wasn't he?"

"I do not know," Juan answered. "I told the boy what would happen to him if he lied—De Soto's dogs would tear him to pieces and crunch his bones. He understood that, I know. Still, he said he would guide us."

"De Soto and the treasurer see in the boy's gestures only what they want to see," Gallegos muttered and stamped off.

It was true, men usually saw what they wanted to see. As for Juan, he saw only an Indian boy, so frightened and despairing that he probably did not know himself quite what he was saying, only wanting to go home. Such a frightened boy Juan himself had been at Ucita's court, so many years ago.

So many years ago. Now when he thought about home, Juan Ortiz thought about his hut, close to Pooy's.

# CHAPTER NINETEEN

# A Battle for a Bed

It was the third of March, 1540, when the expedition left winter quarters in Apalache for its second year of exploration in Florida. The young Indian guide led the column eastward. Gold was what the soldiers talked about most, as Juan remembered them talking when they left Ucita the year before. Gold! Riches! Treasure! The province of the woman ruler lay before them like the Gates of Paradise, as if changing the gender of the Indian ruler would change their luck and would turn grains of maize into rubies and emeralds.

Juan knew this was the Adelantado's work. He had not been idle during the winter months but had kept gold in everyone's thoughts and treasure in every rumor.

However, the caciques of the many villages through which they traveled had never heard of any woman ruler or gold mines. The soldiers began to grumble, to talk of turning back. They looked with suspicion on the Indian guide. He must be lying.

But De Soto gave no sign of discouragement. He exhorted the troops and encouraged his officers.

Often he raged at the guide, for the boy never was sure of the way. De Soto threatened to throw him to the dogs, and he had him chained at night so he would not run away. In the daytime the boy shook and trembled so much that he had difficulty staying on his feet, much less choosing a trail to follow. He stumbled along, holding to Ortiz's saddle. Juan talked to him encouragingly.

The army chanced upon a town called Patofa, which had little food to offer them. The soldiers were so hungry that they fought each other over the few village dogs. Those who won found dog stew delicious. The others did without and tightened their belts. Juan helped himself to greens and roots he found in the woods. But he could not persuade his companions to share his meals.

While here, the guide suddenly began to moan. His body jerked convulsively, and his head rolled this way and that. Froth bubbled from his lips. Falling to the ground, he thrashed about wildly.

"He is mad!" cried a lancer.

"He is possessed by the devil!" shouted another. "Fetch the priest! Fetch the priest!"

One of the priests was nearby and came running. He made the sign of the cross over the guide, sprinkled him with holy water, and said many prayers and incantations. The boy wailed and struggled the harder.

"O Satan, thou enemy of faith, thou root of evil, leave this youth and possess him no more," chanted the priest. He laid his hands on the guide's head and called out, "Satan, thou unclean spirit, I exorcise thee in the name of Jesus Christ."

The boy screamed shrilly and lay still. The priest said, "The demon is gone," and began to pray. Most of the soldiers joined in. They looked frightened.

Since the guide was too weak to walk, Ortiz placed him on his horse and held him there. Soon came the order to march once again. Ortiz mounted, and the boy sat behind, clasping the Spaniard feebly around the waist.

By the end of April the soldiers had forgotten gold and could talk of nothing but food. They were lost among pines, tall, straight, thick trees that closed around them, league after league, in threatening silence and gloom. De Soto kept the men moving as long as he could without food; then some of the hundreds of pigs were slaughtered and their meat rationed daily to the soldiers.

Slowly and steadily eastward they went until at last they reached a large town called Cofitachiqui. A woman did indeed rule over it. The Indian guide was so relieved that he was proven truthful that he asked to be baptised. He was and received the name Pedro and continued with the expedition as a servant.

The cacica was slender and beautiful and greatly respected by all of her subjects. Warriors and young girls constantly attended her. Juan could tell she was a woman of discretion and of queenly heart. Her graceful manner reminded him of Acuera, though she hardly seemed as fair as Acuera, who would always be to him the loveliest of all New World maidens.

There was no gold in Cofitachiqui, but pearls were discovered in wooden coffins in the temples of the dead, buried as an offering with former rulers. The cacica gave De Soto and his officers permission to take the pearls. With chests of these, and with much food, the army continued on its way.

Now the trails were easy to follow, for they had been much traveled by the Indians. Town after town gave the army food and hurried it away, saying that gold and a great quantity of food waited in the next province. North they traveled through a lofty mountain range and then westward through its outlying foothills.

When De Soto led them south across flat, sandy country through August and September, the soldiers realized that their route since leaving Apalache had described a huge circle across the land. This made them speculate whether the Adelantado had at last despaired of finding gold and was heading for the sea and the harbor at Achuse, where the brigantine would be waiting for them. Most hoped this was true, for they were weary of strange places and the multitudes of natives.

Cheerful at the thought of leaving Florida at last, the soldiers did not complain as usual at the commander for hurrying them over the trail. The weather was hot, the way dusty, and the autumn countryside a spectacle of blazing colors, but they felt or saw none of this, so filled were they with the hope of the expedition's end.

Only Juan found this hope of leaving difficult to comprehend. Leave this wild, beautiful land he had come to love? Leave behind forever the wilderness, Florida, the New World life in which he found contentment? He was not certain he could bring himself to go with the other Spaniards, back to a life he had almost forgotten and which had most likely forgotten him.

One morning they approached the fortified town of Mauvila. Camp Master Moscoso wanted to go around it since he had learned through spies that all the Indians of the area were inside, armed and ready to fight the Spaniards.

"Let us avoid the town," suggested Moscoso to the Adelantado. "Then we can be a good many leagues beyond by nightfall and can sleep unharmed and safe in the woods."

"I am impatient with sleeping out," answered De Soto. "I will bed in the town this night."

However, the town made it plain it did not want to have anything to do with the Christians, and De Soto ordered an attack. Juan was grieved for the soldiers. In all their months in Florida not a fight before this had ever involved assaulting a palisaded town. This one was formidable, the walls being built of thick tree trunks embedded in the earth with protected places along the top of the wall for the Indian bowman. How could the Adelantado expect to capture such a strong fort?

All that morning and into the afternoon the battle raged, bloody and fierce. Finally, one lone warrior was left on the palisade wall. He taunted the Spaniards and shot his arrows one by one at them. When they were gone, he called out one last curse and, taking his bowstring, hanged himself from the wall.

The fighting was over, but the Adelantado's desire to sleep one night under a roof had cost the army a high price. Twenty-two Spaniards lost their lives assaulting the town and setting fire to it, while hundreds of others were badly wounded by the Indians' arrows. A dozen horses were slain, and that was a bitter misfortune also.

There was more lost than blood and lives, for the Indian bearers had placed their burdens against the town's walls and fled inside to have their chains filed and so help in the fight. With the burning of the palisades, the Spaniards' clothing, food, and weapons went up in flames. The sacramental wine and the mold to make the holy wafers were ruined. Destroyed also were the chests of pearls—the only treasure to show for two years of exploration. It was almost more than the soldiers could bear.

While Spanish weapons accounted for hundreds and hundreds of dead, that many more savages threw themselves into the flames of the burning houses to perish rather than be taken captive. Few warriors in the town even tried to escape. Still, no one claimed that such a great slaughter of infidels was a Christian victory.

The army stayed near Mauvila for almost a month, while the wounded recovered and weapons were repaired. During this time Juan Ortiz was busy with the few captives and those Indians brought in from the countryside by cavalry raids. De Soto wanted to know where the many trails leading from Mauvila went and how prosperous the nearby provinces were.

One day a soldier escorted an Indian runner to Juan, saying he had just arrived in camp and seemed to have a message of some kind. Ortiz took him to a spring for water and got some corn cakes hot from the ashes for him. He had been running for days and had not taken time for food.

The runner came from the harbor at Achuse, where a Spanish ship waited. Would the soldiers return there with him and take the ship? He was to take a message back, telling De Soto's decision.

When the messenger finished eating, Ortiz led him to the Adelantado's camp at the edge of an oak wood. His tent had burned in the Mauvila fire, and now he and his servants slept under the trees with what few possessions had been saved.

An Indian girl squatted to one side skinning a rabbit. De Soto's page poked about in a simmering pot. He lifted with a spoon a string of intestines and, grimacing, flung them into the bushes. He turned and spoke angrily in Spanish to the girl, who laughed and shrugged her shoulders.

A tailor, propped against a tree, sat on a saddle as he patched one of De Soto's jerkins. The chamberlain was seated beside him talking. Ortiz inquired for the Adelantado and was told he had gone to the spring back of the thicket.

Juan and the Indian went in that direction and met De Soto. The interpreter told him about the message.

His face darkened, and the features shrank as if all his blood and flesh had been sucked away. "Go to the ship and sail back to Cuba!" he repeated in a voice flat and harsh with anger. "Go back to Cuba a failure to be laughed at and mocked by every *peon* and *caballero!* No! No! I will never leave Florida until my hands are full of the gold I came here to find."

"The Indian says around the Achuse harbor there is fine land," Ortiz said softly. "The men might go there to farm, at least for a while."

"Let rabbits farm there. I have no patience for founding a settlement and administering a new colony," snapped De Soto. "I am a commander."

He crossed his arms and glared at Juan and the native. "The chests of pearls I would have sent back to Cuba," he said. "They would have spoken more and better words than I. The pearls would have brought soldiers speeding here to enlist in the army. Now . . . ruined by the fire . . . gone!" His jaw worked as he ground his teeth together.

Then suddenly he grabbed Ortiz fiercely by the shoulder, his face leaning into the interpreter's. "No one knows this message?" he asked. "That the ship waits?"

"I came straight to you," answered Juan. "Not even the guard who brought the native to me heard our talk."

"How far away is the harbor?" De Soto wanted to know. Juan asked the Indian and told the commander it was three days' travel south.

"Three days for him," the Adelantado remarked. "More for us as weary as we are from the battle. The ship is too far away to help us. Here it is the middle of November, the season cold, food scarce. We have no time to go to the seacoast. We must find sustenance near at hand."

Juan could see that his mind was made up, that he would continue his search for that rich kingdom he felt he was destined to find; that rich kingdom that not one of the soldiers who had looked with him for hundreds and hundreds of leagues believed in any longer; that rich kingdom that De Soto needed to bring himself credit in the eyes of the world. Juan would not mind traveling with the Adelantado on across Florida. He looked forward to it, in fact, but the soldiers did not share his pleasure. They yearned to leave this land with fierce passion.

"Juan Ortiz," the Adelantado said, "since I rescued you from the infidels, I have treated you fairly. My demands have not been unreasonable. Now, I want you to swear to me that you will not mention a word to the soldiers about this ship."

It was a little thing he asked, and Juan said he would keep the matter to himself. After all, he had never been a spiller of secrets and had no confidants among the soldiers.

"You have no cause to worry, Adelantado," Juan assured him. "I will tell no one."

"Good." De Soto nodded. He fumbled at his waist and drew a knife from his belt. The sunlight flashed on it as he handed it to the native. "Tell him, Ortiz, it is for bringing me the message. Get him away at once before the other Indians question him. He can tell the ship's captain we go on."

He walked away, and Juan watched his retreating back. Sooner or later, somehow or other, Juan knew, the soldiers would discover what had happened. When they found out that De Soto had denied them the chance to go home, they might mutiny.

And if they mutinied, De Soto would crumble and fall like a long-rusted suit of armor. Inside his skin nothing lived. Somewhere in the wilderness his dream of vast wealth and fame had fallen to bits, mouldered to dust. Perhaps someday Hernando de Soto would be buried in Spain, but in truth he had already died long since in the haunting twilight under the great trees of Florida.

# CHAPTER TWENTY

ᗧᗤ ᗧᗤ ᗧᗤ

# Two Heads Saved

Juan did not believe that De Soto had enough control over his troops to pull them together into a fighting force again and continue the exploration, but he had. At the end of November he led them north to seek winter quarters.

The soldiers followed, each knowing from their Indians that the sea lay in the opposite direction and that a ship had been sighted there. Since masters and slaves knew little of each other's tongues, whose ship it was, whether it was wrecked on the beach or had only come and gone—these things the Spaniards could not learn from their slaves. The soldiers suspected a great deal and they grumbled much, but they did not defy the commander's orders to march inland.

The natives fought the Spaniards most of the way to the town of Chicaça, where De Soto chose to spend the cold months. The Indians deserted their small, clean town as the whites approached it. It was located on top of a ridge with a fine view of the surrounding sa-

vannas and scattered groves. These woodlands con-
tained beech, chestnut, and walnut trees, and the
ground underneath was covered with fallen nuts,
which made a welcome addition to the soldiers' bean-
and-maize diet. There were also many oak woods
about the town, and the pigs gorged and fattened on
the acorns.

With plenty of food and pleasant quarters, the soldiers were satisfied to idle away the days. Juan, however, roamed the woods and creek banks, hunting with
his bow.

One day as he returned with a gutted doe across his
shoulder, he was stopped by a group of Chicaça Indians, whose town was nearby. They wanted to know
how it was that a Spaniard used an Indian bow and,
pointing to his tattoos, how he came to have them. He
was not fluent in their language, but he answered the
Chicaça as best he could.

They understood. Did he not want to leave these
strange white people and live once more with Indians,
they asked. He would be welcome in their own tribe.
Juan smiled. It was a compliment. Perhaps he would
come to live among them. He would like it very much.
Not now, he would not come now. But when his task
was over—

They went on to the camp with Juan, for they came
to complain to De Soto about the thieving of his soldiers. Ortiz escorted them to the commander's dwelling. He was outside talking to Captain Gallegos and
Camp Master Moscoso.

After the greeting formalities were over, Juan explained why the Chicaças were there. "My soldiers thieves?" De Soto scowled. "I will not have it. Find the guilty ones."

He sent the two officers through the camp, and Gallegos soon returned with De Soto's page and his chamberlain and the skins and shawls they had stolen. The goods were given back to the Indians. The two offenders stood trembling before their master. They knew their punishment would not be light.

"Gallegos, take them to a priest and let him hear their confessions," the commander said, "for this afternoon they shall be beheaded for this last sin of theirs."

"Beheaded!" uttered Gallegos, thunderstruck.

"Take them away," De Soto said, then turned to Juan. "Tell the natives what I have ordered so that they may tell their cacique." There was no need for translation. The Indians already understood, from the sound of the Adelantado's voice and the looks on the faces of the culprits. Juan had only begun to speak when they set out to tell their tribesmen.

"Excellency," said Captain Gallegos. "Will you not reconsider? Is not beheading extreme for thieving?"

"I caught three Chicaças stealing my pigs last week," he answered. "Two I killed; the other's hands I cut off and sent him to his leader to warn him to leave us alone. Should I not treat my own in the same fashion after stealing from the Indians?" He mounted the steps to the dwelling on top of the mound and disappeared into it.

"Ortiz, he is mad!" Gallegos exclaimed. He looked at the young page quietly weeping and at the chamberlain standing stiff and pasty-faced. "We must think of some way to save them."

Juan could see how the soldiers were reacting to the sentence. Death, for stealing from the infidel savages? Why, the men sometimes had stolen from each other, from white Christians, and had gotten only a few blows of the fist if they were found out. To be put to death for stealing a few furs from the dark savages—it was too much!

That afternoon an appalled silence lay heavily over the town. Soldiers moved about in the sunshine aimlessly or gathered in the square to stand and wait. It was very oppressive to Juan. He had given away most of his morning's kill. He would get out of the village and hunt again.

Gallegos came running up to his hut. "Ortiz," he said, panting. "The Chicaça cacique is here to see the execution. Listen to me. I have a plan."

The captain wanted Juan to send the cacique away, telling him that the Spanish religion forbade those of other faiths to witness an execution. Then he must go to De Soto and say that the cacique had come to the town to say that the Spaniards had not offended him by stealing and, since the goods were returned, it would be a favor to him if the offenders were freed.

It was an admirable solution. Everyone was satisfied. De Soto was relieved, Juan could tell. He freed the offenders with a terrible tongue lashing, and that was that. The soldiers were pleased, and life went on at winter quarters as if nothing had happened. It had all been settled by the interpreter.

Perhaps not even De Soto or Gallegos realized what power Juan Ortiz held over the expedition. Of all the Spaniards, he and he alone nearly always knew what the Indians were saying. Of all the Christians, he and he alone could convey messages to the Indians.

True that he did not always speak the tongue of each tribe the army encountered. But he could generally speak a tongue that someone among the slaves understood. And he did not think of the Indians as alien creatures, the way the other Spaniards did. He had lived among them long enough to think and feel as the natives did. He could discern often what motives and meanings lay behind the words they said.

Every day he had the opportunity to guide the Spaniards wrong or to mislead the Indians about their purposes and intentions. He could tempt De Soto in this direction or that with tales of gold and treasure, or send him thither and yon fleeing rumors of dangers and deserts.

Now before them lay a great river, bigger than Europe's largest river, wide as the sea, full of huge fish and poisonous snakes and treacherous currents. De Soto had most certainly made up his mind to cross. For the past month the craftsmen had been hollowing out four vast tree trunks to make pirogues that would carry the horses and soldiers across.

Yet surely Juan Ortiz could change De Soto's mind if he so desired. The interpreter knew that most of the soldiers earnestly wished that something would happen to prevent the crossing. Not one of them believed any longer that there was wealth to be found in this spiteful country. They asked only to turn back while they could still travel, to go to the harbor at Achuse and from there return to Cuba and then to Spain. They were only pushing on so that the Adelantado need not admit defeat.

But Juan Ortiz had little enough to turn back to, little enough reason to deceive the commander. If the leader wished to cross, why not cross? And the other side of the river? What kind of country would that be?

In the pale drifts of fog the cavalrymen led their animals down the bank and into the boats. Four lancers and their mounts were first to cross in each pirogue, and a few infantrymen, in case the Indians contested their landing. Juan Ortiz was to go with them to offer greetings to the natives if they were peaceful.

Into the dark current slipped the pirogues. Egrets soared in and out of the misty morning light. A bird called far off, the horses snorted in fear, and Juan peered toward the other bank. What lay ahead?

# INTERLUDE VIII

What lay ahead for Juan Ortiz across the great river (the Mississippi) was death. The expedition took up winter quarters in the Indian town of Autiamque in December 1541. It marched away from there March 6, 1542. Sometime during that period Ortiz died. Not one of the four chroniclers of the expedition mentions the exact date or the cause of his death. He must have been at that time about thirty-two years old, for Garcilaso de la Vega wrote in his history that Juan was eighteen when he first became a captive of Ucita in 1528.

Only the most outstanding followers of De Soto turn up in the four accounts of the expedition. And after his initial rescue and the story of his captivity, Ortiz is infrequently mentioned in them. However, there is no reason to doubt that he played a major role in helping the expedition penetrate the unknown green curtain of southern America. As the only Christian interpreter, he had to be at De Soto's side whenever and wherever the Adelantado confronted the natives.

His passing brought forth eulogies from two of the

expedition's historians. Garcilaso de la Vega calls him "that faithful interpreter," adding, "Throughout the entire exploration he had served no less with his forces and strength than with his tongue, for he was an excellent soldier and of much help on all occasions."

The Knight of Elvas says Ortiz's death was "a loss to the Governor greatly regretted; for without an interpreter, not knowing whither he was travelling, Soto feared to enter the country, lest he might get lost."

Elvas goes on to tell of the army's hardships without Juan after they left Autiamque: "The death was so great a hindrance to our going, whether on discovery or out of the country, that to learn of the Indians what would have been rendered in four words, it became necessary to have the whole day: and oftener than otherwise the very opposite was understood of what we asked; so that many times the road we travelled one day, or sometimes two or three days, would have to be returned over, wandering up and down, lost in thickets."

As so often happens, a man's death underlines his true value while alive, emphasizes that his services which had once been taken lightly and for granted were of vital importance. Thus it was with Juan Ortiz. Gone and missed.

Surely he was given a Christian burial by one of the many priests still with the expedition. Though De Soto was ailing, De Soto would have ordered the proper ceremonies for Juan Ortiz.

But it must have seemed a strange laying-out, that young man in his Indian dress with his weathered, horribly scarred body, his tattooed arms and face. Perhaps he still wore his hair Timucuan style for convenience in carrying arrows.

Perhaps he would have been more comfortable in a Timucuan style grave, in a death hut such as the one he had guarded at Ucita, and by his side his bow and arrows, the only things of value he possessed, for surely he belonged now more to Florida than to the Spain he had left behind.

The savage wilderness put its mark on him right at the very beginning of his life in the New World, when Ucita tied him, spread-eagle, on the *barbacoa* and roasted his back and legs. And later when among the Timucuans he acquired those beautifying tattoos.

There was more to the power of the wilderness than such outward brands. The new-found land surely squeezed his heart with wonder and pricked his imagination. The dark and majestic woods, the distant, mysterious smoky-violet mountains, the bronze-gold savannas of stiff grass, all as full of secrets as were the silent comings and goings of furred and feathered and scaly creatures—surely they beckoned him westward, always westward, away from that part which lay behind him, beyond the Ocean Sea's rim.

Inside and out, America marked him—the first wilderness tattoo on its first pioneer. And it would go on marking those pioneers who followed Juan Ortiz across the vast stretches of this New World in later times.

Autiamque was located in south-central Arkansas on some part of the Ouachita River, experts believe. From there the expedition moved southward across Louisiana toward the great river. On May 21, 1542, Hernando de Soto died and was sewn into a sack of sand and buried in the waters of the Mississippi.

Camp Master Moscoso had been chosen by the Adelantado as his successor to get the expedition safely out of the wilderness. And he did. For months the Spaniards wandered, lost and enduring great hardships, but at length the survivors arrived at Panico, Mexico, on September 10, 1543, in vessels they had built themselves.

Elvas says: "Just as the Christians arrived at the town, in their clothing of deer-skin, dressed and dyed black, consisting of frock, hose, and shoes, they all went directly to the church, to pray and return thanks for their miraculous preservation."

About three hundred members of the expedition reached Mexico. They brought back from their four years of wilderness wanderings only their lives and what contentment they might find in saying that they were the first white men to look upon southern America.

# OBITUARY

## Juan Ortiz—First American Pioneer

*Born 1510 (?)—Died 1542 (?)*

Juan Ortiz died without ever seeing his home in Spain again, but there is no reason to suppose that he died any the more unhappily for that. In the New World he had learned that neither riches nor fine weapons nor the familiar streets of home are necessary to a good and happy life. He had learned to be self-reliant, to trust that the future would turn out well, to make the best of things, and to meet whatever happened with courage. He died among Spaniards and Christians.

But had he never been rescued from the Indians, had he died among the Timucuans, it is likely he would have regarded his life as a good and satisfying one.

Surely he deserves to be called the first American pioneer.

# SELECTED BIBLIOGRAPHY

SOURCES FOR JUAN ORTIZ AND THE DE SOTO EXPEDITION:
Bourne, Edward Gaylord, editor. *Narratives of the Career of Hernando de Soto.* Translated by Buckingham Smith. Volume I: "The Discovery of the Province of Florida" by a Knight of Elvas. Volume II: "A Relation of the Conquest of Florida" by Luys Hernandez de Biedma and "An Account of De Soto's Expedition" based on the diary of Rodrigo Ranjel, his Private Secretary, and translated from Oviedo's *Historia General y Natural de las Indias.* New York: A. S. Barnes & Co., 1904.

Garcilaso de la Vega, el Inca. *The Florida of the Inca.* Translated and edited by John Grier Varner and Jeannette Johnson Varner. Austin: University of Texas Press, 1951.

COMMENTARY ON THE DE SOTO EXPEDITION:
*Final Report of the United States De Soto Expedition Commission,* John R. Swanton, Chairman. Washington: Government Printing Office, 1939.

SOUTHERN INDIAN TRIBES:

Lorant, Stefan, editor and annotator. *The New World, the First Pictures of America.* New York: Duell, Sloan and Pearce, 1965.

Lowery, Woodbury. *The Spanish Settlements within the Present Limits of the United States.* Volume I. New York: G. P. Putnam's Sons, 1901.

Swanton, John R. *Early History of the Creek Indians and Their Neighbors.* Bureau of American Ethnology, Bulletin 73. Washington: Government Printing Office, 1922.

————. *The Indians of the Southeastern United States.* Bureau of American Ethnology, Bulletin 137. Washington: Government Printing Office, 1946.

BIOGRAPHY:

Maynard, Theodore. *De Soto and the Conquistadores.* New York: Longmans, Green and Co., 1930.